Ski and Snowshoe Trails in the Adirondacks

Ski and Snowshoe Trails in the Adirondacks

BY TONY GOODWIN

Adirondack Mountain Club, Inc.

Lake George, New York

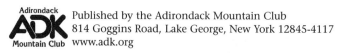 Published by the Adirondack Mountain Club
814 Goggins Road, Lake George, New York 12845-4117
www.adk.org

The Adirondack Mountain Club (ADK) is dedicated to the protection and responsible recreational use of the New York State Forest Preserve, parks, and other wild lands and waters. The Club, founded in 1922, is a member-directed organization committed to public service and stewardship. ADK employs a balanced approach to outdoor recreation, advocacy, environmental education, and natural resource conservation.

Design and layout by Ann Hough
Cover photographs © 2003 by Carl E. Heilman II
Page maps by Forest Glen Enterprises, except as noted. Trip 11 map by Therese Brosseau. Preliminary maps for Trips 8, 9, 17, 18, 42, and 47 by Jeffrey Caron. Most of the preceding are based on maps originally developed by Karen Brooks.

Library of Congress Cataloging-in-Publication Data

Goodwin, Tony, 1949–
    Ski and snowshoe trails in the Adirondacks / by Tony Goodwin.
      p. cm.
    Includes index.
    ISBN 978-1-931951-02-9 (alk. paper)
    1. Cross-country skiing—New York (State)—Adirondack Park—Guidebooks. 2. Snowshoes and snowshoeing—New York (State)—Adirondack Park—Guidebooks. 3. Adirondack Park (N.Y.)—Guidebooks. I. Title.

GV854.6.A35 G66 2002
796.93'09747'5—dc21
                                                                    2002038554
Printed in the United States

12   4 5 6 7 8 9 10 11 12

Dedication

This book is dedicated to ALMY COGGESHALL, who was writing about how and where to cross-country ski long before many of us took our first stride. A leader of ski tours for many years, Almy wrote an instructional book, *Ski Touring in the Northeastern United States* (1965), plus two guidebooks: *Nordic Skiing Trails in New York State* (1977) and *Twenty-Five Ski Tours in the Adirondacks* (1979). Although the equipment has changed in appearance over the past 30 years and these books are now out of print, Almy's descriptions of how to glide through the winter landscape are as good as any in print today. His two guidebooks were the first to introduce many of the tours described in this book. Almy's work broadened the horizons for winter travel for all of us.

Acknowledgments

The trips described in this guide cover nearly every corner of the vast Adirondack Park, an area no one person can ever fully know. The author would therefore like to thank the authors and editors, past and present, of the ADK Forest Preserve Series for the data they have gathered over the years. Each description contained in this guide is the author's, but the earlier work of the FPS authors and editors made it possible to find appropriate trips and describe them in great detail.

I also would like to thank John Kettlewell, ADK publications director, for his advice in reshaping this guide to appeal to a wider audience of winter users. Thanks are also due to Stephen T. Buckbee, who produced the page maps, and to Andrea Masters who, as copy editor, honed the descriptions to near perfection.

Finally, I owe great thanks to my family who tolerated, even if they never quite understood, my desire to drive to the far reaches of the Adirondacks to ski, snowshoe, or hike a trip for inclusion in this guide.

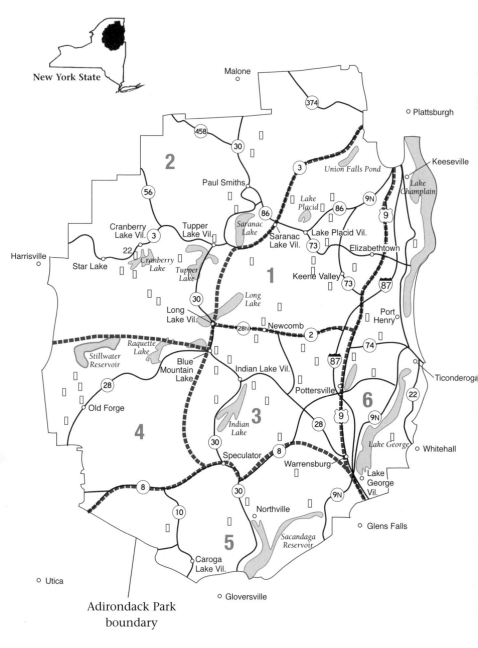

New York State

Malone

Plattsburgh

374

458

30

2

3   Union Falls Pond   Keeseville

Paul Smiths   Lake
Champlain

56   Lake
Placid   9N

86   86   9

Saranac   Lake Placid Vil.   Elizabethtown

Cranberry   3   Tupper
Lake Vil.   Lake Vil.   Saranac   73
Lake Vil.

Harrisville   22   Cranberry   Tupper   Keene Valley   73   87
Lake   Lake   **1**

Star Lake   Long
Lake   Port
Henry

30   Long
Lake Vil.   28N   Newcomb   2

Stillwater   Raquette   74
Reservoir   Lake   Blue   87
Mountain   Indian Lake Vil.
28   Lake

Old Forge   Pottersville   **6**   Ticonderoga

4   Indian
Lake   28   9   22

9N

8   Lake George   Whitehall
Speculator

30   Warrensburg   Lake
George
Vil.

8   30   9N

10   Northville   Glens Falls

5   Sacandaga
Reservoir

Utica   Caroga
Lake Vil.

Gloversville

Adirondack Park
boundary

✳ Trip descriptions in this guide
1. High Peaks Region   4. West-Central Region
2. Northern Region   5. Southern Region
3. Central Region   6. Eastern Region

Contents

Crossing Avalanche Lake

Before You Go

The Adirondacks offer practically limitless opportunities for both cross-country skiing and snowshoeing. Most of the trails described in summer hiking guides are suitable for snowshoeing, and many are skiable as well. This guide draws on the knowledge and experience gained by skiers and snowshoers over the past several decades to highlight trips throughout the Adirondack Park that have proved particularly well-suited to these methods of travel.

Nearly all of these trips are also described in the Adirondack Mountain Club (ADK) Forest Preserve Series guidebooks, and this book is divided into regions corresponding to those covered by the series. One can thus refer to each region's guide to find additional trips in a particular area. This book introduces each region with information on the type of terrain offered, a list of cross-country ski centers (most of which now welcome snowshoers as well), and likely sources of information on snow conditions.

The trips selected range from short trips for novices to ascents of peaks, including Mount Marcy, for the experienced. (Those skiers looking for the greater challenge of steep mountain descents should consult Dave Goodman's excellent guide, *Backcountry Skiing Adventures: Vermont and New York*. Snowshoers can find many additional challenges in ADK's comprehensive Forest Preserve Series of hiking guides.) All of the ski tours can, of course, be done on snowshoes as well, but this guide also includes eleven trips whose slopes are too steep or whose trails are too narrow for skiing. These trips are excellent introductions to the possibilities for snowshoeing in each region.

Winter Travel in the Adirondacks

This guide assumes that its users already possess at least a moderate amount of outdoor experience in winter. (John Dunn's *Winterwise*, published by ADK, is an excellent resource for those who wish to learn more about being active in the outdoors in winter.) It therefore makes no attempt to teach one how to ski or snowshoe. Mention is made of recommended equipment, techniques, or ability required for a particular trip, but it is up to each user to determine his or her own ability and to choose the correct equipment for a particular trip.

Aside from the potential of being far more remote than other mountainous areas of the Northeast, Adirondack skiing and snowshoeing

Minimizing Your Impact on Winter Trails

The Adirondack Mountain Club supports the Leave No Trace principles of low-impact trail use. In keeping with that philosophy, I recommend the following for day-trippers on winter trails in the Adirondacks.

1. Plan ahead and prepare. Applicable for any backcountry trip, this recommendation is especially important in winter. Know the terrain, any hazards, and the weather for the day. Be prepared, with the gear and clothing you carry, for an unexpected night out. Leave an itinerary and anticipated time of return and stick to it. Consult map and compass frequently so as to be sure of your location and thereby avoid a night out. A true emergency in winter may be justification for cutting boughs and burning wood that is not dead and down, but it is far better to plan and prepare and thereby avoid an emergency situation.

2. Dispose of waste properly. Packing out everything you brought in should go without saying. Use privies if at all possible, which may require shoveling the entrance. If no privy is available, the absolute best practice is to also pack out any solid human waste. If that is not possible, bury it at least 200 feet from any water in a deep snow well. Use a map to locate water sources, which may not be as evident in winter. The extra distance from water (compared to summer recommendations) is required because human waste remains frozen until spring melt—at which point it will be on the surface and subject to washing into any nearby water. Snow is an effective alternative to toilet paper and has the advantage of not having to be packed out.

3. Respect wildlife. Many animals, deer in particular, are especially vulnerable in winter. Observe them from a distance, and use a telephoto lens for close-up shots. Attempting to approach wildlife may cause them to startle and run, using up precious reserves of the stored energy that must last them through the winter. Dogs must also be controlled so that they do not chase wildlife. Under no circumstances should one feed wildllife. Not only could this be dangerous, but it helps create a dependence on human-provided food.

4. Be considerate of other visitors. A discussion of Sharing the Winter Trail appears later in this introduction. In addition, one should control dogs, especially where skiers descending at higher speeds may be encountered, and check for any special regulations pertaining to dogs in the area one plans to visit. Remember to pack out or bury all pet waste. In this guide, dogs must be leashed on Trips 1,2,3,7, and 12. Dogs are prohibited on Trip 6.

opportunities are much like those found elsewhere. The weather can be severe at times, with sudden thirty- to forty-degree (Fahrenheit) drops in temperature possible at any time during the winter. A warm spell with rain can be followed by colder weather and treacherous frozen crust. Likewise, a heavy snowfall can slow one's pace to a near crawl and necessitate a change of plans. Do not set out with the idea that the temperature and snow conditions will remain the same all day, and always have an alternate plan in the event that the proposed trip is not feasible.

Emergencies

Gear. None of the trips described in this guide are patrolled, so you are on your own as far as safety and rescue are concerned. On the longer trips especially, each skier should carry enough clothing to keep warm for an extended period of inactivity in the event that an injury forces the group to stop. One should also carry sufficient supplies to stay alive if forced to spend the night. Someone in the party should have a foam pad to insulate any injured person from the snow, and a tarp or space blanket. Though bulky to carry, a sleeping bag is desirable as it can be many hours before help arrives. A bit of plumber's tape, a few radiator hose clamps, some wire, and some nylon cord are also useful both for field repair of equipment and for constructing a makeshift toboggan on which to move an injured member of the party.

Procedures. See sidebar, page 14.

Equipment

Skis. On all of the trips described one should expect unbroken snow and no prepared tracks. Racing or training skis are not appropriate, but all the described trips can and commonly are done on either light touring or touring skis. Although some may prefer the extra control and flotation of mountain skis with metal edges, the trade-off is that these heavier, wider skis make for slower progress on easier terrain. Very wide "bushwhacker"-type skis have become popular with some skiers, but these are very slow on flatter sections. Furthermore, in deep, unbroken snow anyone with such wide skis will essentially break trail the entire distance—unless, of course, everyone in the party has the same skis. For the steeper trips such as Mount Marcy or any of those trips designated

Emergency Procedures

Backcountry rescues are the responsibility of Department of Environmental Conservation (DEC) forest rangers. Names and telephone numbers of the local rangers are usually posted at major trailheads along with the DEC's emergency dispatch number. For the Adirondacks that number is 518-891-0235. Calling this dispatch number is preferable to calling 911 since emergency requests to 911 can end up being transferred through several other agencies before the report reaches the DEC.

In recent years, cell phones have figured in several emergency situations and have helped to reduce the time required to summon help. However, cell phone coverage in the Adirondacks is spotty at best, especially in the valleys, and one should never count on making contact. Additionally, cold temperatures may significantly shorten battery life. Therefore, do not assume that help will always be just a phone call away, and even in the best of circumstances it can still be a long, cold wait until help arrives. *Cell phones should never be a substitute for proper planning and equipment.*

When reporting an emergency situation (after making sure that it really *is* an emergency), provide the dispatcher with a call-back number in the event more information is needed. And just to be on the safe side, call back at some point to check; often in marginal areas one can make an outgoing call, but an incoming call will not "ring in."

as snowshoe trips, a pair of climbing skins may be useful.

Poles. Avoid poles with small, racing-style baskets; otherwise any sturdy touring pole will do.

Boots. On extended trips, warmth is perhaps the most important consideration, followed by control and support. Although technology will continue to evolve in this area, boots that continue to meet the above criteria best are the old favorite 75 mm, three-pin boots. A boot that comes up at least to the ankle is preferred, with gaiters and overboots added for additional warmth as needed.

Snowshoes. Currently the most popular and available snowshoes have an aluminum frame with neoprene decking. They usually come with a built-in creeper (metal claw) for traction on hard surfaces. The smallest models are suitable only for packed surfaces such as those found at ski touring centers or on the most popular "trunk" trails, such as the approach to Marcy Dam from Adirondak Loj. For most of the snowshoe trips described, all but the lightest individuals should choose a snowshoe at least ten inches wide and twenty-four to thirty inches long.

Clothing. Volumes have been written about the merits of various types of winter clothing, but the one common thread is that cotton is to be avoided. Wool or synthetic pile are desirable because they do not soak up water and retain most of their insulating capability even when wet. A windproof outer layer for both top and bottom is also important—especially if the proposed trip includes any open areas, such as summits or lakes.

Map and compass. As on any backcountry trip, one should always carry a compass and the appropriate topographic map(s). Trails in winter can be more difficult to find and follow, so there is a greater possibility than in summer that one might need to use a map and compass to regain the proper route. Each trip description references the map or maps needed for that trip.

Snowfall and Snow Conditions

The trips described in this book are not on packed or groomed trails, so skiers and snowshoers must deal with conditions as nature has created them.

Amounts. Snowfall amounts can vary tremendously from one part of the Adirondacks to another. The western and southern edges generally receive more snow than the northern and eastern areas. Average annual snowfall at Old Forge, for example, is between 180 and 200 inches, tailing off to 150 inches at Blue Mountain Lake, Cranberry Lake, Northville, and Newcomb. North Creek and Paul Smiths average around 120 inches, while the Lake Placid area averages just over 100 inches. The Champlain Valley and much of the eastern Adirondacks receive from seventy to ninety inches.

These differences are most apparent in low-snow years, when areas such as Old Forge, Newcomb, Paul Smiths, or Northville might have passably good conditions while much of the rest of the Northeast has virtually no snow at all. It pays to call around. On any given winter's day, even in winters with little snowfall, at least a few of the trips in this book are likely to have sufficient snow cover. The other significant factor in snowfall is elevation. Areas above two thousand feet receive considerably more snow, and above three thousand feet the difference in snow depth can be pronounced—up to more than one foot for each one thousand feet of additional elevation. Most consider this gain in snow depth an advantage, but remember that more snow also means slower trail breaking.

Surface conditions. Fresh powder is nice, but users should be prepared for the full range of conditions and the possibility that things can change even during the course

Truck Trails

The term seems counterintuitive: Since when does a truck need a trail? Actually, these are foot trails with a history—and, as a consequence, a different appearance from a typical Adirondack foot trail.

Truck trails were constructed in the 1930s for fire protection and in the 1950s to salvage downed timber—also done in the name of fire protection—after the hurricane of 1950. They were called "trails" because the construction of roads was forbidden in the Forest Preserve. Today, truck trails are quite different from woods roads or tote roads in that they are of a more recent construction, are surfaced with gravel, and are drained by extensive ditches and culverts.

For skiers knowledgeable about the Adirondacks, the term connotes an easy-to-ski route, even when minimal snow is present.

of an afternoon tour. The ski difficulty rating for each trip assumes either cold powder or soft spring conditions. Icy conditions raise the difficulty of a given ski trip, and snowshoe creepers may be inadequate, requiring the use of full crampons. Breakable crust may make a trip practically impossible to ski (and certainly not very enjoyable), while snowshoers may find their pace slowed to less than one mile per hour.

Travel on ice. Several of the trips described in this guide cross lakes, and it must be each user's own judgment at the time whether the ice is safe. Be aware that after a major thaw even seemingly thick ice can be dangerously weak, and be especially cautious near inlets and outlets of lakes at all times.

Another problem on lakes is that sometimes water will seep up through cracks in the ice and create a layer of slush under the snow that will freeze on skis or snowshoes. The leader may often skim over these areas, but followers should watch for gray patches forming in the tracks and avoid them. Carry a good scraper (and possibly an extra in case someone in the party has forgotten) so that the group can resume movement as soon as possible in the event that everyone ices up.

Public and Private Land

The Adirondack Park comprises over six million acres. A little more than forty-eight percent (if one counts the surfaces of publicly accessible lakes), or 2.9 million acres, is owned by the State of New York and known as the Adirondack Forest Preserve. Since 1894, Forest Preserve lands have been constitutionally protected to remain "forever wild." These lands may not be leased to private individuals nor may the timber on them be cut or sold. Over the years, specific amendments to the state constitution have permitted the use of Forest Preserve lands for projects such as I-87 (the Adirondack Northway) and the ski centers on Whiteface and Gore Mountains. Development on the rest of the Forest Preserve has been limited to primitive trails and other facilities, such as lean-tos, to facilitate public recreation.

In 1972 the State Land Master Plan further classified Forest Preserve lands as either Wilderness, Primitive, Wild Forest, or Intensive Use. For cross-country skiers and snowshoers, the major significance of these classifications is that snowmobile trails may exist on lands classified as Wild Forest but not in Wilderness or Primitive areas. Mechanical grooming of trails is permitted only in the Intensive Use areas at Mt. Van Hoevenberg and Gore Mountain. All other cross-country ski centers in the Adirondacks are on private land.

The topographic or National Geographic Trails Illustrated maps that accompany ADK's Forest Preserve Series guides delineate private and public land and identify the classification of each public parcel. Descriptions in this guide will mention the classification of the land where it has any importance for the skier or snowshoer.

One must be aware that parts of many of these tours—particularly the trailhead areas—are on private land. This demands the utmost courtesy and respect for the landowner since many access points to public lands exist only by tradition and the continuing generosity of landowners. Park vehicles so they cannot possibly block any private access or space needed for a plow to turn around. It should go without saying that camping and the building of fires are prohibited on private land. There also are special restrictions on certain pieces of private land, such as no dogs allowed on the road to Lower Ausable Lake (Trip 6).

Snowmobile Trails

On public (Forest Preserve) land in the Adirondacks and Catskills, snowmobiles are restricted to those trails specifically designated for snowmobiling. There are no designated snowmobile trails in areas classified Wilderness or Primitive, but currently there are about 900 miles of designated snowmobile trails in areas classified Wild Forest. Additionally, there are many more miles of established snowmobile trails on private land.

A few of the trips in this guide follow designated snowmobile trails, and the introduction to each trip gives some indication of the average level of use by snowmobilers. The snowmobile trails included in this guide do not usually receive heavy use, but on any given day one may have to share the trail with some machines. When skiing on snowmobile trails, use extra caution—especially on downhills—in the event one encounters a snowmobile. When encountering snowmobiles operating on a designated trail, common courtesy should prevail regardless of one's personal feelings about this form of motorized recreation. If one suspects illegal snowmobile use, report the registration numbers to a forest ranger. In general, illegal snowmobile use on public lands has not been a common problem.

How to Use This Guide

Arrangement of trips. Trips are presented by region and located by number on a page map at the beginning of each section.

Maps. The heading for each trip includes a list of topographic maps for that trip. If the trip is on an ADK map, that map is referenced first, followed by the corresponding USGS maps. The ADK maps include information on private and public land while also showing trail data that is updated more frequently than on the USGS maps. ADK maps also combine several separate USGS sheets into one map, making them usually more economical than the same coverage on USGS maps.

The USGS now covers most of the Adirondacks with a series of metric

Legend

‑ ‑ ‑ ⌐ ˏ ‑ ‑ ´	Ski/snowshoe trail
═══════	Woods road
🗼	Fire tower
⬛	Lean-to
■	Outpost or lodge
⛺	State campground
▲	Summit
P	Parking
9N	State or local highway
9	U.S. highway
87	Interstate highway
	Private land
～	Stream or river
	Lake or pond
	Wetland
├─┼─┼─┼─┼─┤	Railroad

unit 7.5- by 15-minute sheets. These USGS maps are on a scale of 1:25,000 and are referenced as "metric series" in the trip headings. Some areas in the northern and southern edges of the Adirondacks are covered by older 7.5 minute USGS maps printed on a scale of 1:24,000. This type of map is referenced as a "7.5 minute sheet." The older 15 minute USGS series maps at 1:62,500 scale are no longer commercially available and therefore are not listed.

Page maps have been provided in this book for each tour. These and the text will get you to the trailhead and familiarize you with significant features of the tour. However, one should carry the relevant topographic map, and only the text should be relied upon for exact distance figures.

Distances. These are derived using either a surveyor's wheel or a pedometer. In instances where such measurements are not available, distances have been derived from estimates on the trail and map measurements.

Times. No attempt has been made to estimate times for any trip because differing snow conditions, the variable of breaking trail in different snow depths, and widely divergent skiing abilities make it impossible to establish a standard time against which a skier can reliably compare his or her own time. In general, when skiing in a broken track with powder or similarly fast snow, one should be able to travel a bit faster than a normal summer hiking pace. Snowshoe travel is generally a bit slower than summer hiking. When breaking trail with either skis or snowshoes, however, one's speed can often drop below one mile per hour. The best advice is to start early, know when the sun sets, and watch the time carefully. On point-to-point or loop trips, be prepared to retreat along the broken track at an agreed-upon time—even if you are more than halfway to the destination.

Difficulty ratings. The terms used to rate the skiing and snowshoeing difficulty of each trip are explained below. Whichever rating appears first at the beginning of the description indicates the method of travel best suited for the trip.

These ratings address the technical skill required to negotiate the terrain on a particular trip. They do not take into account the overall length and difficulty of a trip or the special experience required to travel above timberline.

In general, one should be able to snowshoe or ski for as many hours as one is comfortable hiking. Note, however, that this statement does not take into consideration the significant extra energy required to get up from repeated falls should one end up on a trip with terrain that is beyond one's abilities. With fatigue, one's technique—whether on skis or snowshoes—deteriorates in a frustrating, if not frightening, downward spiral. If in doubt, start with shorter, easier trips to avoid getting into a potentially dangerous situation.

With regard to skiers, perhaps the best definitions of *novice*, *intermediate*, and *expert* come from John Frado, former manager of Northfield Mountain Cross-Country Center in Massachusetts. A novice, says Frado, "needs a darn good snowplow," while an intermediate "has a darn good snowplow." A true expert, by contrast, "can do a darn good snowplow while eating his lunch." A more detailed, if less colorful, set of definitions for both skiers and snowshoers follows:

Beginner:
SKIER—A person with little or no skiing experience, able to negotiate only the gentlest of hills, up or down.
SNOWSHOER—A person with little or no snowshoeing experience, able to negotiate gradual hills only.

Novice:
SKIER—A person who has cross-country skied several times, can climb gradual hills, and feels comfortable coasting down gradual hills. Limited ability to control speed or stop with a snowplow.
SNOWSHOER—A person who has completed several successful backcountry trips and can climb and descend moderate slopes without slipping or falling.

Intermediate:
SKIER—A stronger skier who can climb moderate hills straight up and steeper hills with a herringbone. Can also control speed on downhills with a snowplow and make turns on moderate terrain.
SNOWSHOER—An experienced snowshoer who can climb moderately steep slopes and descend without falling. A ski pole or poles may be helpful on such terrain.

Expert:
SKIER—A thoroughly experienced skier who can handle steeper terrain, including turning and stopping under a variety of snow conditions.
SNOWSHOER—A thoroughly experienced snowshoer who can ascend the steepest terrain, including kicking steps if necessary. Ski poles or an ice ax plus crampons are required on such terrain.

Breaking Trail and Sharing the Trail

Breaking trail. In the past few decades, winter use in the Adirondacks has increased to the point that many of the most popular trips seem to be broken out within a day or so of any storm. On many routes trail breaking is easier than it used to be because one is only dealing with the most recent storm and not a whole winter's accumulation of snow. Furthermore, if one finds that they are the first travelers after a storm, often another party will catch up and share the heavy work. Even so, frequent changes of the lead are important to keep any one member of the party from becoming too tired or overheated.

Sharing the trail. With the great increase in winter use, many trails are now used by both skiers and snowshoers, sometimes resulting in friction between the two groups of users. Skiers, in particular, have been known to become upset when snowshoers flatten out skied-in tracks. This really shouldn't be a problem. With deep snow especially, a packed snowshoe track makes a good base for a skied-in track while also packing an area to the side for the poles. In an ideal world, and on a road-width trail with a moderate amount (two to eight inches) of new snow, snowshoers would be doing the skiers a favor by making their own track. This assumes, however, that the skiers who were first carefully skied to one side to leave room for a second set of tracks. In any event, no skier should become too upset with any snowshoer because—think about it— how often has one seen skiers make a separate track if snowshoers were first on the trail after a snowfall? Ultimately, both groups of users are out there for the same reason.

Postholers. The bane of both skiers and snowshoers (more so in recent years, it seems) are those who either don't bring skis or snowshoes or don't bother to put them on. These "postholers" or "bare-booters" can quickly turn a nice smooth, easy-to-walk or -ski trail into a bumpy mess that is difficult or dangerous to negotiate. Since 2001, regulations specific to the High Peaks Wilderness Area have provided that ski or snowshoe use is required when there is more than eight inches of snow on the ground. Forest rangers can issue tickets to enforce this regulation. Unfortunately, the regulation has yet to reduce the number of post-holers encountered. Experience has also shown that angry confronta-tions don't do much good either. My advice is to note the holes being made, mention the regulation, and move on.

High Peaks Region

The High Peak region offers some of the most spectacular cross-country ski and snowshoe terrain to be found anywhere in the Northeast. Partly for this reason and partly because of its familiarity to summer hikers, the High Peaks region is also the most popular place for winter recreationists. This does not mean, however, that this region always has the best conditions (it often doesn't) or that there is no comparable experience elsewhere. One shouldn't limit one's skiing or snowshoeing to the High Peaks region exclusively. Nonetheless, a winter trip up Mt Marcy or through Avalanche Pass is an experience to be savored.

Note that special restrictions for dogs pertain in this region. Of the trips described in this guide, dogs must be leashed on Trips 1, 2, 3, 7, and 12. Dogs are prohibited on Trip 6.

The High Peaks region has a number of developed facilities at or near its periphery that cater to snowshoers and cross-country skiers. The closest is Adirondak Loj, operated by ADK, which features a network of ski and snowshoe trails, a wide practice slope, and a warming building (ADK's High Peaks Information Center), where staff offer rentals plus advice on weather and trail conditions. There is a parking charge, money that not only helps maintain the parking lot, but also supports ADK's broader trail maintenance and education programs. ADK members receive a seventy-five percent discount on parking. The Loj also has recorded weather information describing current conditions twenty-four hours a day (see telephone numbers below). The Adirondack Ski Touring Council is a source specifically devoted to ski conditions throughout the region.

Like the Adirondacks as a whole, the southern and western sides of the High Peaks receive the most snow, and it is not uncommon to have nearly bare ground in Lake Placid and at the Loj while Newcomb has over a foot of snow and great skiing. The Adirondack Park Visitor Interpretive Center in Newcomb (one of two "VICs" in the Park) offers information on local conditions plus some snowshoeing on its own trail system.

High Peaks Region

Trail Ratings for Skiers

Beginner
11. Moose Pond

Novice
2. Newcomb Lake and
   Camp Santanoni
6. Lower Ausable Lake
9. Connery Pond to
   Whiteface Landing

Novice-Intermediate
10. Whiteface Mountain
    Memorial Highway

Intermediate
3. Raquette Falls
4. Jackrabbit Trail
8. Owen, Copperas,
   and Winch Ponds

Intermediate-Expert
1. Marcy Dam, Avalanche Lake,
   and Lake Colden
12. Flowed Lands and Lake Colden
    from Upper Works

Expert
5. Owl Head Lookout
7. Mt. Marcy

(map labels) 3 · Union Falls Pond · 11 · Lake Placid · 9 · 10 · 9N · 86 · 9 · 8 · 86 · Saranac Lake Vil. · Lake Placid Vil. · 4 · 9N · Elizabethtown · 3 · 1 · 7 · Keene Valley · 5 · 6 · 73 · 1 · Long Lake · 12 · 28N · 2 · Newcomb · Long Lake Vil. · 2

Trail Ratings for Snowshoers

Beginner
2. Newcomb Lake and
   Camp Santanoni
6. Lower Ausable Lake
9. Connery Pond to
   Whiteface Landing
11. Moose Pond

Novice
4. Jackrabbit Trail
8. Owen, Copperas, and
   Winch Ponds
10. Whiteface Mountain
    Memorial Highway

Intermediate
1. Marcy Dam, Avalanche Lake,
   and Lake Colden
3. Raquette Falls
5. Owl Head Lookout
12. Flowed Lands and Lake Colden
    from Upper Works

Expert
7. Mt. Marcy

High Peaks Region Cross-Country Ski Centers and Sites
Adirondak Loj, Lake Placid: 518-523-3441 (office),
    518-523-3518 (weather line)
Adirondack Park Visitor Center, Newcomb: 518-582-2000
Adirondack Ski Touring Council, Lake Placid: 518-523-1365
Cascade Cross-Country Ski Center, Lake Placid: 518-523-9605
Mt. Van Hoevenberg cross-country ski center, Lake Placid: 518-523-2811
Whiteface Inn Nordic Center, Lake Placid 518-523-7888

1. Marcy Dam, Avalanche Lake, and Lake Colden

Distance: 14.0 mi (22.4 km) round-trip to Lake Colden
Elevation change: 930 ft (284 m)
High-point elevation: 2985 ft (910 m)
Difficulty: Ski, intermediate-expert; snowshoe, intermediate
Maps: Page 27. ADK High Peaks Region; USGS Mount Marcy and
    Keene Valley metric series

With spectacular scenery, easy access, and a virtual guarantee of a broken track, Lake Colden has for many years been a popular destination
for both skiers and snowshoers. (The 8.0 mi round-trip to Marcy Dam on
the truck trail is a very pleasant ski trip in its own right. Most snowshoers, however, prefer to make the trip to Marcy Dam via the 4.6 mi
round-trip hiking trail from the Loj.) To reach Lake Colden there is 0.5
mi of steep terrain on the north side of Avalanche Pass, but any reason-
ably strong skier can negotiate this pitch without too much trouble.
Snowshoers generally continue to use the summer hiking trail to climb
and descend the north side of Avalanche Pass.

Although some skiers and most snowshoers heading for Marcy Dam
prefer the shorter approach from Adirondak Loj, this trip is described
using the wide, well-graded Marcy Dam Truck Trail from South
Meadows. This route is 1.6 mi longer because the South Meadow Road
(now Meadow Lane) is no longer plowed but is often skiable many
weeks before the hiking trail is skiable.

▶The truck trail approach is found by turning off NY 73, 4.0 mi
southeast of Lake Placid or approximately eleven miles from Keene.
Three and eight-tenths of a mile from NY 73, Meadow Lane diverges left
and is marked by a small sign. Park here, but be careful not to block the
entrance in case an emergency vehicle needs to get through.◀
    From Adirondak Loj Road (0.0), heading up Meadow Lane, a gated

road branches right at 0.9 mi and leads 200 yd to the registration station at the former location of the gate and the actual start of the truck trail. From the registration station, the trail is flat for 0.3 mi to a junction with the Mr. Van Ski Trail. (Owing to lack of a bridge over Marcy Brook, it may be difficult to ski to Adirondak Loj.) From this junction, the trail climbs in a series of mostly gentle rolls to Marcy Dam at 3.8 mi. The DEC interior outpost here is not staffed in winter, but there are five lean-tos around the pond. Continuing from the dam and register, one briefly follows the blue-marked trail to Mt. Marcy before turning right and following yellow markers for the gentle climb to Avalanche Camp, which has a lean-to, at 4.9 mi. The next 0.5 mi is often called "Misery Hill," but a series of skier bypasses takes away at least some of the "misery" on the ascent and considerably mitigates the difficulty on the way down. For snowshoers, the shorter hiking trail is the preferred route both up and down.

From Avalanche Camps, the skier's bypass is found by starting left and up the blue-marked trail to Lake Arnold for about two hundred yards and then continuing straight ahead where the Lake Arnold Trail turns sharp left. The ski trail climbs moderately to steeply to a crossing of the hiking trail about one-third mile from Avalanche Camps. Continuing across the hiking trail, the ski trail switchbacks left and recrosses the hiking trail in 300 yd. This is followed by a switchback to the right to rejoin the hiking trail on the flat just before reaching the top of Avalanche Pass at 5.4 mi.

The large and spectacular slide that comes down to the trail at the top of the pass occurred during Hurricane Floyd in 1999. As noted by signs, the slide is steep enough to present the possibility of an avalanche. To reduce the chance of a human-triggered avalanche, the DEC prohibits any skiing or climbing on this slide. Although the chance of a spontaneous avalanche is remote, prudence dictates only pausing to look and not settling down for a picnic at this scenic location.

Once over the pass, the trail narrows and twists between boulders and under ice-covered cliffs before descending in a few short pitches to Avalanche Lake at 6.0 mi. (This trail often has a good deal of traffic in both directions. Skiers should thus stay in good control when descending.) The spectacular cliffs rising up on both sides make a natural wind tunnel, so be prepared to don a windproof layer and perhaps goggles and face mask for the 0.5 mi trip across the lake. Entering the woods at 6.5 mi, the trail descends to a junction and register at 6.8 mi, where the hiking trail splits to go along the east and west shores of Lake Colden. The easiest skiing and snowshoeing, however, is found by continuing straight ahead and following the former telephone line (marked with an occasional yellow DEC ski trail disk) to the north end of Lake Colden at 7.0 mi.

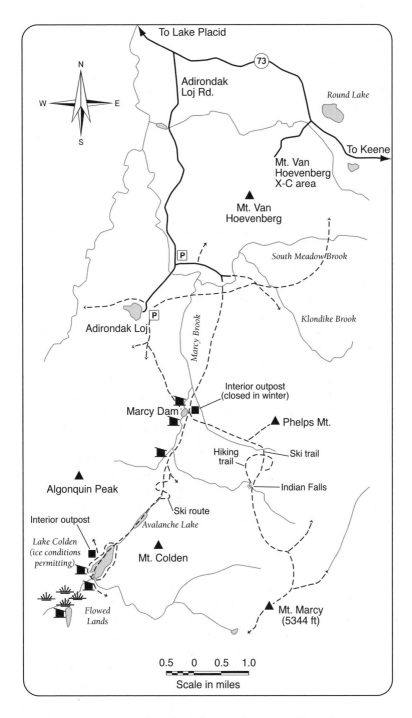

*Marcy Dam, Avalanche Lake, and Lake Colden (Trip 1)
and Mt. Marcy (Trip 7)*

A DEC interior outpost (usually staffed in winter) is located midway down the west shore. There are also two lean-tos with spectacular views at the far end of the lake that offer a good place to rest and eat lunch. To continue on to Flowed Lands, pass to the left of the dam at the south end of the lake and immediately cross the Opalescent River. Then continue south for 0.3 mi on a trail that parallels the left bank of the river, passing two lean-tos and proceeding to the north end of Flowed Lands. If continuing on to Upper Works, head south-southwest across the open area to find the trail at Calamity Lean-tos.

2. Newcomb Lake and Camp Santanoni

Distance: 9.4 mi (15.2 km) round-trip
Difficulty: Ski, novice; snowshoe, beginner
Maps: ADK High Peaks (partial; north from junction at 2.2 mi); USGS Santanoni Peak and Newcomb metric series

Offering gentle grades, a smooth road, and a beautiful destination, this has been a popular trip ever since the state acquired this parcel of land in 1973. In some of the recent snow-drought years, the Newcomb area has often been the only place in the entire Northeast where there was any good cross-country skiing. In addition to the trip described below, there are many other longer trips possible, including a 13.5 mi round-trip to Moose Pond and several overnight trip possibilities on the horse trail system along the Cold River and on to Coreys or Lake Placid.

▶ The access to Newcomb Lake is found at the west end of the village of Newcomb (0.3 mi west of Newcomb Town Hall) and is marked with a sign for the Santanoni Preserve. A narrow road leads 0.3 mi across a bridge and up past the gatehouse, where there is parking to the right. ◀

From the gate and register (0.0 mi), the road is flat for 0.9 mi to some old farm buildings, after which a short climb leads to a view of the Santanoni Range at 1.1 mi. A gentle descent and climb brings the road to a junction at 2.2 mi. (Road left leads 4.5 mi to Moose Pond.) Continuing to climb gently, the road levels off and begins to descend gently at 3.2 mi, passing a junction with the hiking trail along the south side of Newcomb Lake at 3.7 mi. The road continues its gentle descent and crosses Newcomb Lake on a bridge at 4.4 mi before swinging left along the north shore to Camp Santanoni at 4.7 mi. Reaching this classic Adirondack Great Camp is simple and straightforward, but this property and camp have both a long history and a present situation that is

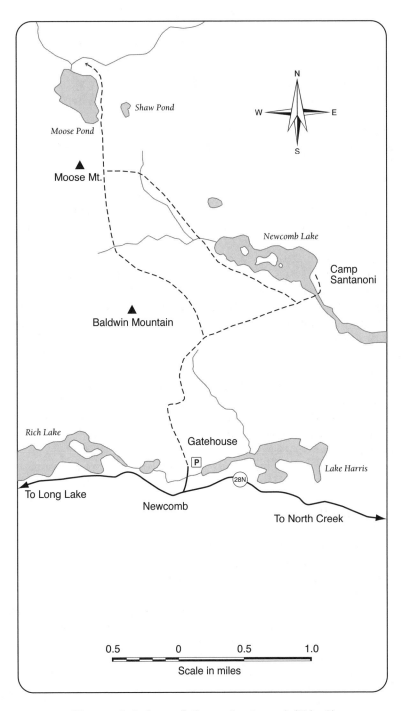

Newcomb Lake and Camp Santanoni (Trip 2)

anything but simple and straightforward. Completed in 1893 by Robert C. Pruyn of Albany, Camp Santanoni was the centerpiece of his 12,000 acre Santanoni Preserve. Robert H. Robertson, then a prominent New York City architect, designed the camp. In 1903 Delano and Aldrich, another New York architectural firm, designed the farm complex, with William Delano himself designing the gatehouse that was built two years later. Robert Pruyn continued to enjoy his property until his death in 1934. In 1950, Pruyn's estate offered the entire property to New York State for $145,000. At the time, no funds were available, so in 1953 the Melvin family bought the property.

Later the Melvin family also made several offers to sell the property to the State, but it was not until 1972 that the Nature Conservancy facilitated the transfer. Initially, all buildings were to be torn down in accordance with DEC policy for structures on property acquired as part of the Forest Preserve. An understandable reluctance to destroy such a large and unique structure, however, led to its designation as a National Historic Site. Following this designation, the DEC and the Adirondack Park Agency created the Camp Santanoni Historic Area, a 32 acre parcel of land that includes a gatehouse complex, farm complex, Great Camp complex, and Newcomb Lake Road. Thus Camp Santanoni and the other buildings still stand, and preservation work has begun on some of the most critically deteriorated structures. The exact use for all of the structures in this complex has yet to be determined, but the Unit Management Plan for the Camp Santanoni Historic Area (completed in August 2000) considers skiing and snowshoeing to be the primary winter uses for the Newcomb Lake Road. Thus horse and wagon use, a popular means of summer access, is prohibited during snow season.

3. Raquette Falls

Distance: 10.6 mi (17.1 km) round-trip
Difficulty: Ski, intermediate; snowshoe, intermediate
Maps: ADK High Peaks Region; USGS Tupper Lake metric series

This justly popular trip reaches a spectacular destination with relatively little effort and only a few short stretches during which the going is difficult. This area often has better snow conditions than areas closer to the High Peaks, and this trip's popularity means there will usually be a good broken track within a day or so of any storm. The start of this trip is also the starting point for longer trips to Duck Hole, Shattuck

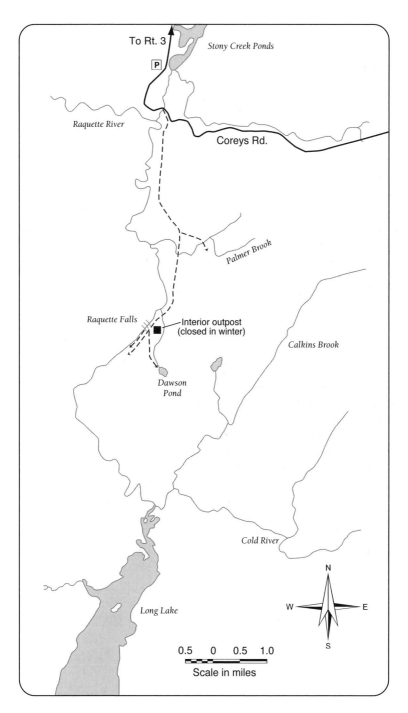

To Rt. 3

P

Stony Creek Ponds

Raquette River

Coreys Rd.

Palmer Brook

Raquette Falls

Interior outpost
(closed in winter)

Calkins Brook

*Dawson
Pond*

Cold River

Long Lake

N

W ◆ E

S

0.5   0   0.5   1.0

Scale in miles

Raquette Falls (Trip 3)

Clearing, and Newcomb.

▶ The start is at the end of Coreys Road off NY 3, 12.7 mi west of the traffic light in the center of Saranac Lake Village and 2.7 mi east of the junction of NY 3 and NY 30, east of Tupper Lake. The road is marked with a large DEC sign reading "High Peaks via Duck Hole." Coreys Road is plowed for 1.5 mi to the marked end of town plowing, where there is some limited parking. The road is privately plowed beyond this point, but one proceeds entirely at one's own risk. ◀

Starting at the end of plowing (0.0 mi), you cross Stony Creek on a bridge at 1.0 mi and at 1.3 mi there is a small parking area on the right with a trail register box. Turning right and passing the register, the trail begins climbing gently. At 3.3 mi the trail crosses a small brook and climbs more steeply for 100 yd before coming to a junction with a side trail to Hemlock Hill Lean-to at 3.7 mi. The trail then dips down to a junction at Palmer Brook at 3.8 mi. (The trail going straight leads to Calkins Brook at 8.3 mi and Shattuck Clearing at 12.8 mi.)

Turning right, the trail to Raquette Falls crosses Palmer Brook and begins to climb. (Those following the map closely will be relieved to know that the route does not go over the top of this hill as shown, but skirts to the north and east.) After descending to the edge of a slough of the Raquette River at 4.4 mi, the trail has several small ups and downs before beginning a longer climb to a crest at 5.4 mi. The trail now descends via a series of steep switchbacks, which challenge a skier's proficiency at snowplowing, before reaching the signpost at the canoe carry at 5.8 mi. A DEC interior outpost (not staffed in winter) is up and to the left. To reach the actual falls, continue up the canoe carry approximately one hundred yards and then turn right on a vague trail leading approximately one-third of a mile to a falls at the head of a gorge. With good snow cover, one can continue along this trail to see the entire mile-long section of rapids, with the canoe carry making a good return route. Another worthwhile side trip is Dawson Pond, reached by a 0.7 mi trail that is found at the southeast corner of the large field south of the interior outpost.

4. Jackrabbit Trail

Distance: 24.0 mi (38.7 km), Saranac Lake to Keene
  (some distances estimated)
Elevation change: 940 ft (287 m)
High-point elevation: 2610 ft (796 m), height of land between
  McKenzie Pond and Whiteface Inn Road
Difficulty: Ski, intermediate; snowshoe, novice
Maps: Pages 34, 36, 38, and 41. ADK High Peaks Region;
  ASTC Jackrabbit Trail Map; USGS Lake Placid, Keene Valley,
  and Saranac Lake metric series

Begun in 1986, the Jackrabbit Trail is a unique opportunity for cross-country skiing and snowshoeing. It links populated areas, developed cross-country ski centers, and some longer wilderness sections to make possible a tremendous variety of trips. The construction and maintenance of the Jackrabbit Trail is the major project of the Adirondack Ski Touring Council (ASTC), a membership organization composed of local businesses and trail users. The private-land section of the trail between Cascade Cross-Country Ski Center and the Lake Placid Resort is groomed by these centers and a trail fee is required on this section. As of 2003, one ticket is good at both ski centers. Otherwise, there is no charge for the use of the trail. Snowshoeing is permitted on all sections of the trail. The most popular snowshoe trips are on the Old Mountain Road section, from Whiteface Inn Road to the lean-to, and from McKenzie Pond Road to McKenzie Pond.

The trail is named in honor of Herman "Jackrabbit" Johannsen, a legendary skiing pioneer in the Adirondacks and, later, in Canada. There he constructed the famous Maple Leaf Trail and helped establish the 100 mile, two-day Canadian Ski Marathon. While living and vacationing in Lake Placid between 1916 and 1928, Johannsen laid out some of the original routes used by today's trail. He was also famous for his one-day ski ascents of Marcy starting from Lake Placid—a round-trip of over 30 miles. "Jackrabbit" died in 1987 in his native Norway at age 111, skiing nearly to the time of his death.

Future plans include expansion of the Jackrabbit Trail to Tupper Lake. ASTC publishes an annual map of the Jackrabbit Trail, available free of charge at local ski shops and other businesses or by mail (with self-addressed envelope and postage for two ounces) from: ASTC, P.O. Box 843, Lake Placid, New York 12946. ASTC also provides cross-country ski conditions both by phone (518-523-1365) and on the Lake Placid Visitors Bureau Web site, www.lakeplacid.com.

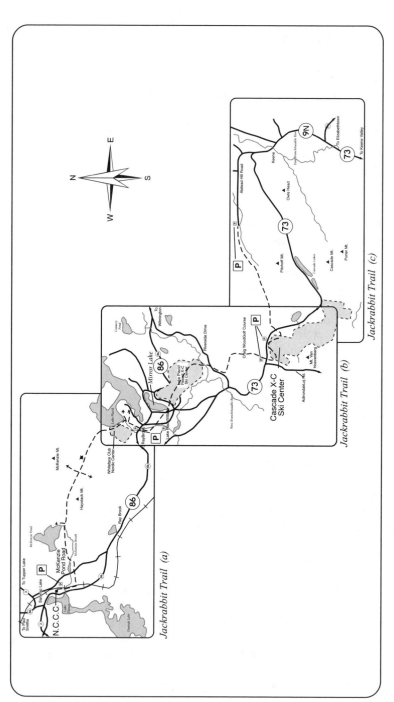

Jackrabbit Trail overview (Trip 4)

▶ One can start from many points on the trail and traverse as much or as little of the trail as one desires, so the following brief description from Saranac Lake to Keene is not the only way to do the trail. Private-land sections of the trail are marked with large red rectangular markers bearing the logo of the Adirondack Ski Touring Council and the Jackrabbit Trail, whereas state land sections are marked with yellow DEC ski trail disks. Distance is given at the start of each major section, with the cumulative total in parentheses at the end. ◀

Saranac Lake to McKenzie Pond Road
1.5 mi (2.4 km); maps on pages 34 and 36

One can start from the town hall via Riverside Park, but the best access point is at the North Country Community College (NCCC) gymnasium, which is found by following the signs from NY 86 in Saranac Lake. From the gymnasium parking lot (0.0 mi), the trail follows the railroad tracks, used seasonally, for 0.5 mi and then turns sharp left and up through a pine grove to join an old snowmobile trail at 0.7 mi. Turning left, the Jackrabbit Trail then follows this snowmobile trail for another 0.8 mi before turning right to McKenzie Pond Road at 1.5 mi.The Jackrabbit Trail resumes on the other side of the road, 100 yd to the right (east). McKenzie Pond Road is the beginning of a 5.5 mi wilderness section and is a popular start/finish point.

McKenzie Pond Road to Whiteface Club Nordic Center
5.5 mi (8.9 km); maps on pages 34 and 36

From McKenzie Pond Road (0.0 mi) the trail is mostly level to a power line. The trail soon leaves the power line by bearing left and down to a small bridge. Continuing on gentle terrain, the trail reaches state land at 0.5 mi, crosses McKenzie Pond Outlet at 1.0 mi, and joins the old truck trail at 1.1 mi. From here, the terrain is flat to McKenzie Pond at 1.9 mi.

From here it is a 1.5 mi continuous climb to a pass between Haystack and McKenzie Mountains. Skied in this direction, it is merely a long climb, but skied in the other direction it requires a bit more than inter-mediate skill to negotiate. (Those who can negotiate this hill, however, consider it one of the finest runs in the Adirondacks.) After cresting the pass, the trail descends moderately to a four-way junction at 4.0 mi. (The red trail right leads to Rt. 86; red trail left leads to the summit of McKenzie Mountain.) Continuing straight ahead on nearly flat terrain, the trail passes a lean-to on the left at 4.5 mi and begins a gradual descent for 0.7 mi to the upper edge of the Whiteface Club Nordic

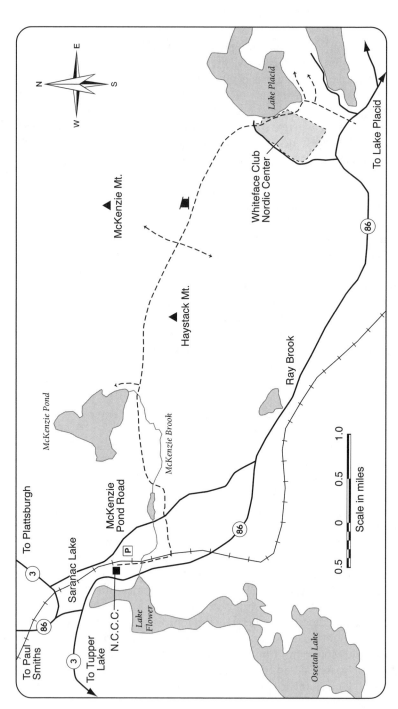

Jackrabbit Trail (Trip 4), map a

Center. From here the descent steepens for the final 0.8 mi to the Whiteface Inn Road at 6.0 mi (7.5 mi from NCCC).

Whiteface Club Nordic Center to Mirror Lake
3.5 mi (5.6 km); maps on pages 34, 36, and 38

The character of the next section of the trail is radically different, as it winds its way around and through the Village of Lake Placid. There are a number of road crossings and just over 0.3 mi of road walking.

To continue, turn right just before reaching Whiteface Inn Road and ski 200 yd to a road crossing opposite the Whiteface Club golf course. (As of 2003, skiers were not charged a trail fee to pass through the golf course. Skiers should be aware that the exact route across the golf course may change as development continues along the edges of the course.)

After crossing the road (0.0 mi), continue straight ahead for 150 yd and turn right and up a gentle hill along the left side of a fairway. At the top of the hill the trail turns left, crosses another two fairways, and comes to a plowed road. Crossing the plowed road, the trail turns sharp left and enters the woods for 50 yd before emerging at the top of a steep descent on another fairway. At the bottom of this hill, the trail follows the left edge of the fairway for 150 yd before swinging sharp left through a short section of woods to another plowed road. This is the end of the golf course, and the trail crosses the plowed road and proceeds to reach a bridge below the Lake Placid dam at 0.8 mi.

Crossing the bridge, the trail swings sharp right for 25 yd, then bears left on a new piece of trail and proceeds mostly on the flat for 0.3 mi to a junction at a small culvert. Continuing straight ahead, some minor ups and downs lead to the parking lot at the Howard Johnson's Restaurant on Saranac Avenue at 1.7 mi. Now crossing Saranac Avenue, most will end up walking for 200 yd to the left of the convenience store and down the road past the Lake Placid Center for the Arts to a bridge across Cold Brook (also known as the Lake Placid Outlet).

Past the bridge, the trail resumes on the right, climbs into the woods, and then swings left to cross the road at 2.2 mi, after which it descends through thick woods to a bridge over the Lake Placid Outlet. After a few more ups and downs, the trail reaches West Valley Road, crosses it, and climbs moderately to the Crowne Plaza at the top of a hill at 3.2 mi. To continue, walk past the Crowne Plaza and descend to the Lake Placid Post Office. Bearing left of the Post Office, cross under the Lake Placid Toboggan Slide to the south end of Mirror Lake at 3.5 mi (11.0 mi from NCCC in Saranac Lake).

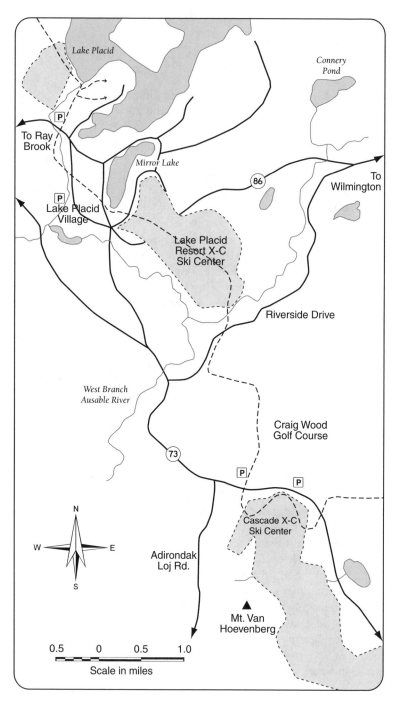

Jackrabbit Trail (Trip 4), map b

Mirror Lake to Cascade Cross-Country Ski Center
6.5 mi (10.5 km); maps on pages 34 and 38

From the south end of Mirror Lake (0.0 mi), the trail crosses Mirror Lake Drive and heads to the right of a large building that was once the employee dormitory of the Lake Placid Club. It then passes to the right of several new condominiums to the golf house that in winter houses the Lake Placid Resort's cross-country center. (The Lake Placid Resort's cross-country center is generally open only weekends and holidays. If open, however, skiers should purchase trail tickets here for the ski to Cascade. Note that ongoing development of this property may cause some of the landmarks mentioned here to change in the next few years.)

From the golf house, the Jackrabbit Trail follows the Bull Run loop down to and across NY 86. Turning left, the trail follows a fairway parallel to the highway to a tall stand of pine trees opposite the Cobble Mountain Lodge. The trail then follows a narrow road down through thick woods and then straight along a flat stretch. At the end of the straight, flat section, the trail bears left to a four-way junction at 2.0 mi from Mirror Lake. Continuing straight through this junction, the Jackrabbit Trail follows the Loggers loop for 300 yd to a sharp right turn onto a new (2003) section of trail. After some short climbs and descents, the trail begins a longer descent to reach a vehicular bridge across the West Branch of the Ausable River at 3.0 mi.

Crossing the bridge and River Road, the trail parallels the road for 0.2 mi and then rejoins the road briefly before turning sharp left and up a side road leading to a private driveway that is plowed but not usually sanded. At 0.2 mi up the private driveway, the trail turns sharp right onto a new section of trail completed in 2001. The trail now descends gently to a bridge and then climbs moderately for 0.3 mi up through a clearing and on to a flat area that has been logged recently. After 0.2 mi of flat terrain, the trail makes a moderate descent to a new bridge with attractive cedar railings and a plaque noting that the bridge was constructed in memory of Theresa Klauck, a former director of the Adirondack Ski Touring Council. From the bridge, a moderate climb brings one to Craig Wood Golf Course.

Crossing the golf course pretty much from north to south, the trail reenters the woods just to the left of a small maintenance shop and climbs gently to NY 73 at 5.0 mi. Crossing NY 73, the Jackrabbit Trail enters the outskirts of the Cascade Cross-Country Ski Center trails and goes through the woods on the flat for nearly 0.3 mi., after which the trail descends along an unplowed road, turns sharp left into thick woods, and continues to descend for another 0.2 mi. A short steep climb leads to a junction with the main part of the Cascade system. Turning sharp left, the Jackrabbit Trail climbs gently for 0.7 mi to the lodge at 6.5 mi (18.0 mi from NCCC in Saranac Lake). (Those starting from Cascade and heading toward Lake Placid must pay a trail fee, but those skiing in from Keene, just to the lodge on the section described below, may do so without charge.)

Cascade Cross-Country Ski Center to Keene
6.0 mi (9.7 km); maps on pages 34, 38, and 41

Past the lodge (0.0 mi), the marked route of the Jackrabbit Trail follows the Beaver Run Trail, a delightful, gentle downhill run to a semi-open marsh. After the marsh, the Jackrabbit Trail exits the Cascade system by turning sharp left at the top of a small hill. (The trail straight ahead leads to the Mt. Van Hoevenberg cross-country ski center, for which a separate trail fee is required.)

Now following a wider trail, the Jackrabbit Trail dips down and up across a small brook, swings sharp left, and continues mostly on the level to NY 73, which is crossed at 1.5 mi. This has long been a popular starting point for those wishing simply to enjoy the mostly downhill 4.5 mi run to Keene. On a busy weekend, however, parking can be a problem here, and skiers are encouraged to start at Cascade Cross-Country Ski Center (0.5 mi west by road). Cascade asks a nominal parking fee, but offers a ski shop, restaurant, and restrooms plus an extra 1.5 mi of skiing.

After crossing NY 73, the Jackrabbit Trail follows a plowed road for 1.0 mi to a very small parking area, with no other parking available along the road. Much of the road is so narrow that meeting vehicles can't pass. The safest choice, therefore, is to park near NY 73 and walk or ski to the end of the plowed road. ASTC hopes to work out a route for a ski trail parallel to the road.

From the end of the town road (2.5 mi from Cascade Cross-Country Ski Center), gentle ups and downs lead to a large beaver pond at 3.3 mi with a spectacular view of Pitchoff's ice-covered cliffs. After a short climb, the trail crests the pass at 3.5 mi and begins a moderate descent followed by a short, steep pitch down to a large beaver pond. Continuing to descend at a gentle grade past this pond, the trail crosses two more small bridges and descends moderately to another old beaver pond at 5.0 mi. After another 0.2 mi of moderate descent, the trail flattens as it approaches the Keene end of the trail at 6.0 mi (24.0 mi from Saranac Lake).

This trailhead is reached by road by turning off NY 73 onto Alstead Hill Road (County Route 40), 0.9 mi up from Keene. Follow Alstead Hill Road past the Bark Eater Inn and to its end, 3.9 mi from Keene. Here

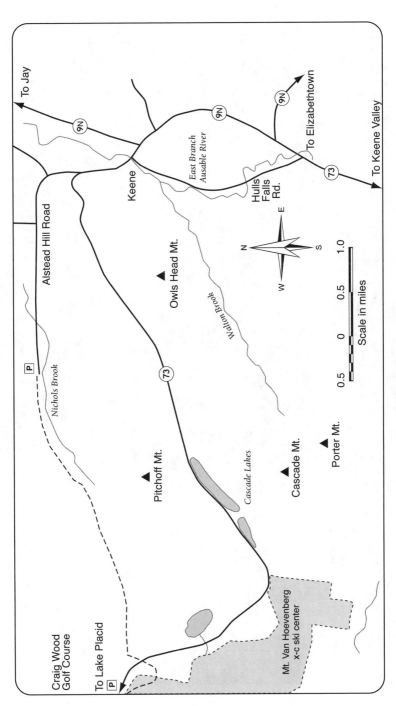

Jackrabbit Trail (Trip 4), map c

The Old Mountain Road, Jackrabbit Trail

there is a small parking lot and Adirondack Rock and River, an inn and guide service.

5. Owl Head Lookout

Distance: 5.4 mi (8.7 km) round-trip
Elevation change: 1220 ft (372 m)
Summit elevation: 2500 ft (762 m)
Difficulty: Snowshoe, intermediate; ski, expert
Maps: ADK High Peaks Region; USGS Elizabethtown metric series

This is an ideal, easy snowshoe trip, but the route also can and has been skied many times over the years. The spectacular summit view, reached with relatively little effort, gives this trip one of the best effort-to-reward ratios in the Adirondacks. The grades are mostly moderate, although the final few yards are quite steep and, whether skiing or snowshoeing, the actual view is likely to be reached with bare boots. Skiing this route requires 1.5–2 ft of snow to be able to leave the trail at key points to swing turns, but snowshoeing requires only the usual six to eight inches of snow.

▶ The start is on NY 9N, 4.5 mi from US 9 in Elizabethtown and 5.5 mi from the junction of NY 9N and NY 73 between Keene and Keene Valley. A large DEC sign marks the trailhead, and the trail itself is marked with red disks. ◀

From the highway (0.0 mi) the trail follows a road a few yards down to a bridge and then diverges left and begins a gentle climb. Snow may be sparse under the thick hemlocks, but within one-half mile the trail reaches state land and an open hardwood forest. The grade eases just before crossing Slide Brook at 1.1 mi, after which there is a short steep pitch up and left to the crest of a ridge. Now the grade moderates as the trail crosses a small brook and goes up through a narrow gully. Leveling out beyond the gully, the trail again begins to climb at 1.8 mi, as it swings right. From here the woods are very open and offer many possibilities for off-trail skiing on the descent.

Going up, the trail climbs in moderate stages to a junction at the crest of a ridge at 2.5 mi. Owl Head Lookout is up and to the left. Snowshoers can usually make it close to the summit before resorting to walking the final few yards to the open rock. Skiers, however, are likely to abandon their skis within 100 yd of the junction and then walk or, depending on snow conditions, wade the final 200 yd to the summit. The 360 degree view from the summit includes the spectacular east face of Giant Mountain plus Rocky Peak, Lake Champlain, Whiteface Mountain, and the Green Mountains of Vermont.

The trail straight ahead at the junction leads to an open meadow in about one-tenth of a mile and then on to the summit of Giant in another 5.0 mi. The open meadow offers both a spectacular view of the Owl Head Lookout cliffs and possibly a more sheltered place for lunch on a windy day. Those looking for a longer and relatively easy trip can continue on toward Giant Mountain. The woods remain generally open and the grades remain moderate to the view at High Bank, 4.1 mi, and to the lean-to at 5.7 mi.

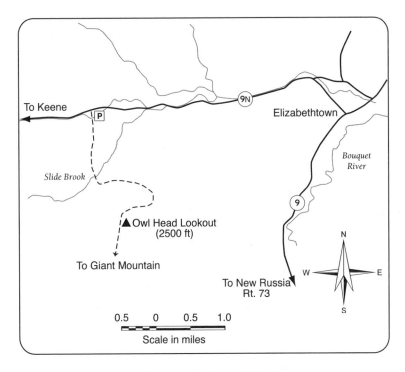

Owl Head Lookout (Trip 5)

6. Lower Ausable Lake

Distance: 8.2 mi (13.2 km) round-trip
Elevation change: 650 ft (198 m)
High-point elevation: 2000 ft (655 m)
Difficulty: Ski, novice; snowshoe, beginner
Maps: ADK High Peaks Region; USGS Keene Valley and Mount Marcy
metric series

A ski up the graded, gravel road to Lower Ausable Lake has long been a popular trip, especially for early season or low-snow conditions. When conditions are right, the ascent is delightful, the scenery spectacular, and the return—in about half the ascent time—pure joy. Mitigating these pluses, however, is the fact that one must park 0.5 mi from the start, that vehicular traffic on the road may make surface conditions less than ideal, and dogs are not permitted under any conditions. Snowshoers can also enjoy this trip but will not get to experience the coast back.

The entire trip is on private land, courtesy of a public easement granted by the Adirondack Mountain Reserve (AMR). This area has been managed for over a century as a game preserve. Hunting has been prohibited since the AMR bought this property in 1886, and a ban on dogs further protects the game. Because of these restrictions, one is far more likely to see deer here than on any other trip in this book.

▶ The public parking area is just off NY 73 on a side road 3.3 mi south of Keene Valley and 5.6 mi north of the junction of US 9 and NY 73 near Exit 30 from I-87. ◀

From the parking area (0.0 mi) head west along the road and eventually along the edge of a golf course for 0.6 mi. Just before the main hotel building, turn left and down a road between two tennis courts for 300 yd to a register at the AMR Gatehouse. Continue straight ahead from the register to an elaborate wooden gate at the actual start of the Lake Road. Landmarks along the road include a crossing of Gill Brook at 1.9 mi (followed by a moderate climb), a small reservoir on the left at 2.5 mi, and the Lower Lake at 4.1 mi.

Owing to frequent strong winds, ice conditions on the lake are usually unfavorable for skiing; in addition, a sign posted at the Gatehouse now states that the surface of the lake is not part of the public trail easement. With good snow, an interesting side trip of 0.5 mi round-trip is possible to Rainbow Falls, which is reached by crossing the bridge just below the Lower Lake dam and following the signs to the base of the falls.

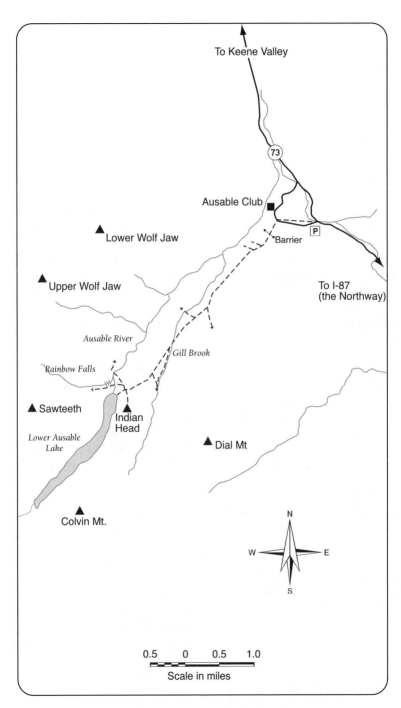

Lower Ausable Lake (Trip 6)

7. Mt. Marcy

Distance: 16.0 mi (25.8 km) round-trip
Elevation change: 3290 ft (1003 m)
Summit elevation: 5344 ft (1629 m)
Difficulty: Ski, expert; snowshoe, expert
Maps: Page 27. ADK High Peaks Region; USGS Keene Valley and
   Mt. Marcy metric series

Though not for everyone, a winter ascent of Mt. Marcy remains one of the Adirondacks's greatest trips. On a warm day with good conditions, the trip can appear deceptively easy; but under no circumstances should the trip be underestimated. Conditions above treeline can be vastly different from those experienced up to the Plateau at 4600 feet. Above timberline, crampons, face mask, and ice ax may be needed to reach the summit. If clouds should close in, a compass and the ability to use it are required to return safely to one's ascent route and avoid straying into the decidedly unfriendly terrain of Panther Gorge. Despite these potential hazards, hundreds make the ascent on skis each winter with many more utilizing snowshoes.

▶ The start is the same as for the Lake Colden trip (Trip 1, page 25). ◀

At Marcy Dam at 3.8 mi bear left to follow the blue-marked Van Hoevenberg trail to Marcy. Under most conditions, winter users will not need to use the high-water bridge across Phelps Brook that is reached at 4.0 mi, but can instead use the regular crossing just beyond. Beyond this crossing, the trail becomes quite rough and wet so that travel can be difficult in low-snow conditions. The trail climbs moderately to the junction with the trail to Phelps Mountain at 4.7 mi and then to a bridge at 5.1 mi.

The next 200 yd beyond the bridge, one of the steepest pitches on the trip, leads to a four-way intersection. The hiking trail goes right, but winter users can continue straight to follow the ski route to Indian Falls, which is reached at 6.1 mi.

After Indian Falls the grade moderates with the trail reaching the top of a hill at 6.5 mi. Now the trail descends gently, swings right, and then steepens briefly at 6.9 mi at a section known as the "Corkscrew," the most challenging pitch of the trail's overall descent. Soon moderating again, the trail works its way up to the crest of the ridge from which one gets the first close-up views of Marcy. Reaching a junction with the yellow-marked Hopkins Trail to Keene Valley at 7.8 mi, the trail then climbs more steeply to the former site of Plateau Lean-to at 8.1 mi. Elevation here is 4600 ft.

Above here the trail narrows and steepens before reaching the junction with the Phelps Trail from Keene Valley at 8.5 mi. In most years the signs at this junction will be totally buried, but snow of this depth allows for some off-trail skiing back down to Plateau. From this junction, the trail goes up over a bare ridge and then climbs moderately up to a narrow vly with an open ridge to the right. The hiking trail ascends this ridge, but most winter users bear left at this point to stay on good snow as long as possible.

Conditions on this final 0.3 mi to the summit vary so widely that no definitive description is possible. The route most commonly used by skiers ascends along the right edge of the large (for the Adirondacks) snowfield and then across the upper part of the snowfield, which usually keeps one on good snow practically to the summit. Snowshoers usually head straight for the summit from the snowfield via the summer hiking trail route.

Do not count on being able to use the summer markings (paint and cairns) to reach and return from the summit. The trail follows a series of ridges between timberline and the summit with the result that anyone who simply heads downhill will be going away from the trail—and probably into Panther Gorge. The magnetic bearing from the summit back to the trail at timberline is 78 degrees, but definitely be prepared to turn back before even reaching the summit if there is any question about the conditions.

8. Owen, Copperas, and Winch Ponds

Distance: 3.8 mi (6.1 km) round-trip
Difficulty: Snowshoe, novice; ski, intermediate
Maps: Page 51. ADK High Peaks Region; USGS Lake Placid metric series

This is an excellent, easy trip for snowshoers, with three pretty ponds as the destinations. The forest in this area was badly damaged by the January 1998 ice storm, but the views of the surrounding peaks from the ponds remain very attractive. The trail is just narrow enough with a few hills steep enough that this trip is better on snowshoes than skis. There are two trailheads, with the southern one recommended because the grades are easier and Owen Pond is more easily reached from the south.

▶ The start is on NY 86 in Wilmington Notch, 5.0 mi east from the junction with NY 73 in Lake Placid and 3.9 mi west of the entrance to Whiteface Mountain Ski Center. The trailhead is marked with a small

DEC sign. ◀

From the road (0.0 mi) the blue-marked trail leads gradually up along the outlet to Owen Pond, reaching the northwest corner of the pond at 0.6 mi. Here one sees the large new slide on Kilburn Mountain that came down in the October 1995 cloudburst. The trail follows the shore of the pond to the northeast corner and then veers away at an easy grade followed by a steeper grade at 1.0 mi. (The bushwhack bypass of this hill is no longer feasible owing to ice storm damage.)

Swinging right at the top of this climb, the trail descends to the former lean-to site on the east shore of Copperas Pond at 1.3 mi. From here one gets an excellent view of Whiteface Mountain and can also see the present lean-to across the pond. (Copperas Pond is quite deep, so the ice may not be as thick early in the season as on Owen Pond.) From the old lean-to site, the trail crosses the outlet and reaches the junction with the trail to Winch Pond at 1.4 mi. Turning right, and now with yellow markers, the trail climbs a short, steep pitch after which a few moderate climbs and descents lead to Winch Pond at 1.9 mi.

9. Connery Pond to Whiteface Landing

Distance: 6.0 mi (9.7 km) round-trip
Difficulty: Ski, novice; snowshoe, beginner
Maps: ADK High Peaks Region; USGS Lake Placid metric series

The skiing on this trip offers just enough challenge to keep experienced skiers from being totally bored while not being terrifying to less experienced skiers. The snowshoeing is easy enough for anyone to handle. For these reasons, this is a justly popular trip to a scenic destination.

▶ The start is on NY 86, 3.1 mi east of the stoplight at the junction of NY 73 and NY 86, and is marked with a DEC sign. Winter parking is at a wide turnout 300 yd farther east and a trail parallel to the highway that allows one to reach the trailhead without walking on the road. The trail follows a private driveway that is sometimes plowed, but in any case it should be skied or snowshoed, not driven. ◀

From the highway (0.0 mi) follow the driveway, marked with red DEC disks. At 0.2 mi continue straight at a junction. At 0.5 mi the marked route bears left and down. About two hundred yards past this turn, a new angler's access trail leads right to the pond. One can either take this trail and then cross to the northwest corner of the pond or continue on

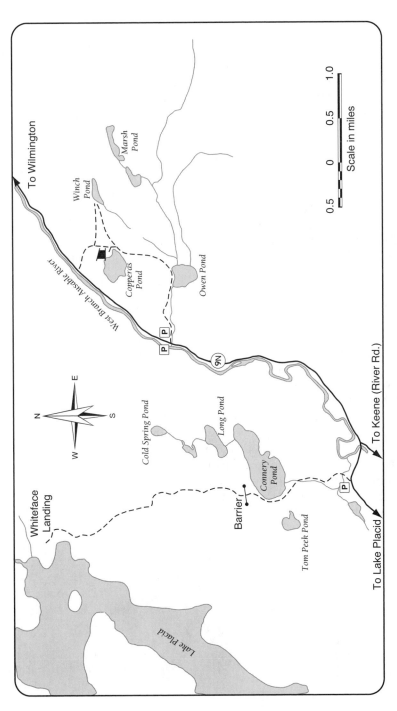

Owen, Copperas, and Winch Ponds (Trip 8) and Connery Pond (Trip 9)

the red-marked trail past a private residence and around the west end of Connery Pond to a gate at the beginning of the truck trail at 0.9 mi. After some flat terrain, the trail climbs gradually to a height of land at 1.9 mi, after which it gently descends to a junction at 3.0 mi. Whiteface Landing at the north end of Lake Placid is a few yards to the left.

10. Whiteface Mountain Memorial Highway

Distance: 11.0 mi (17.7 km) round-trip
Elevation change: 2535 ft (773 m)
Summit elevation: 4867 ft (1483 m)
Difficulty: Ski, novice-intermediate; snowshoe, novice
Maps: ADK High Peaks Region; USGS Lake Placid and Wilmington metric series

On a fair day with good snow conditions, a trip up and down Whiteface Mountain via the highway can seem like a deceptively easy way to make a 4000 ft winter ascent. Under less-than-ideal circumstances, however, surface conditions can be treacherous and the weather just as severe as it can be on any of the peaks above timberline. Furthermore, the wide road and open vistas that start about a mile up the highway mean that one is more exposed to the elements than on a narrow trail. With poor weather conditions and an icy surface, the difficulty ratings for both skiing and snowshoeing increase significantly.

Because of its high altitude and smooth surface, the highway has long been a popular early-season tour or a last resort in low-snow years. After most storms a track is quickly broken out either by other users or by the vehicles of the staff at the Atmospheric Sciences Research Center located just below the tollhouse. After a thaw and freeze cycle, however, this vehicular traffic can leave an icy, rutted, chattery mess. Remember also that the wind can blow all the snow off, exposing the pavement, especially on corners. Grim warnings aside, on more days than not the snow is just fine for this exceptionally scenic trip.

PHIL CORREL

Ascending Whiteface Mountain

▶ The start is at the tollhouse approximately three miles above the village of Wilmington on NY 431. ◀

From the tollhouse (0.0 mi) the first views are at 0.8 mi, followed by a small shed on the left at 1.7 mi. At 3.2 mi the highway crosses the base of a slide and then comes to the first hairpin turn, Lake Placid Turn, at 3.5 mi. With a view of Lake Placid (surprise!) and the steep ridge above leading to the castle and summit, this makes a good destination if the weather is too inclement to continue. Wilmington Turn is reached at 4.5 mi. From here conditions can range from deep drifts to glare ice to the castle at 5.3 mi. From the castle, a summer walkway with railings leads to the summit at 5.5 mi.

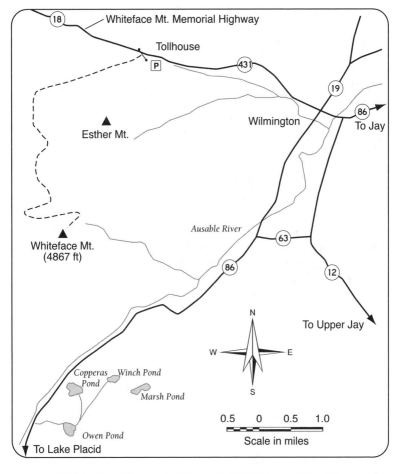

Whiteface Mountain Memorial Highway (Trip 10)

11. Moose Pond

Distance: 3.0 mi (4.8 km) round-trip
Difficulty: Ski, beginner; snowshoe, beginner
Maps: ADK High Peaks Region (partial; Saranac Lake only); USGS
Saranac Lake and Bloomingdale metric series

With its rocky shore and views, Moose Pond is a scenic gem hiding just a short distance from busy NY 3 north of Saranac Lake. This trip follows a wide, graded road that once provided access to several houses on the shore of the pond, so this short trip is an ideal choice for a very first ski or snowshoe outing. The road is also smooth enough that it can be skied with as little as six inches of snow. There is no sign to mark the trailhead and only roadside parking, which can be a problem in a heavy snow year.

▶ The start is located on NY 3, 3.9 mi north of the intersection of NY 3 and NY 86 in Saranac Lake (west of the center of town at a Stewart's Shop). Coming from the north, the start is found 2.2 mi south of the four-way junction in Bloomingdale. ◀

From the highway (0.0 mi) a road leads down between fences for 200 yd to a footbridge over the Saranac River. Turning right after the bridge, the road parallels the river for a few yards and then climbs gently away as it swings to the left. From here to the pond, the road contours along the side of a hill with just a few gentle ups and downs. At 1.4 mi there is a trail to the right that leads more steeply down to the shore of the pond and a popular campsite on a low rocky bluff. One can also continue past the trail for another 150 yd on the road. There may be some downed trees on this piece of road, but it leads to a gentler road proceeding right and down to a chimney that is all that remains of a house. Although there is a good view of Moose and McKenzie Mountains from the rocky bluff, there is an even better view from the center of the pond—ice conditions permitting.

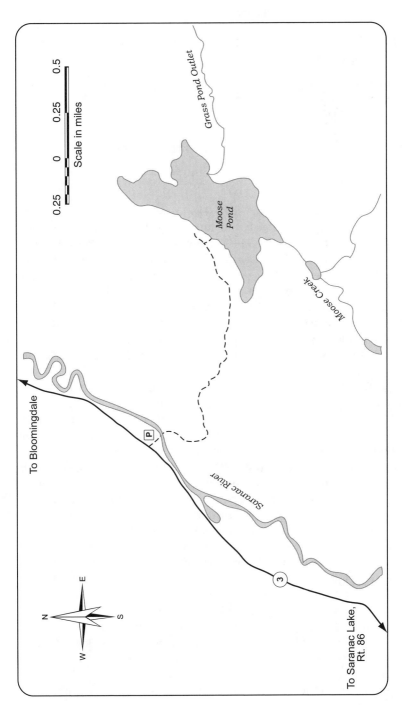

Moose Pond (Trip 11)

12. Flowed Lands and Lake Colden from Upper Works

Distance: 9.4 mi (15.2 km) round-trip to Flowed Lands; 11.2 mi (18.1 km) round-trip to Lake Colden
Elevation change: 965 ft (294 m)
High-point elevation: 2765 ft (843 m)
Difficulty: Ski, intermediate-expert; snowshoe, intermediate
Maps: ADK High Peaks Region; USGS Mount Marcy and Santanoni Peak metric series

The spectacular view from Flowed Lands of Mount Colden and the MacIntyre Range combined with interesting (but not too interesting) skiing make this tour a favorite of many skiers. Nonetheless, this route probably is used by more snowshoers than skiers. When done as a point-to-point traverse with Lake Colden from the north (Trip 1), this is one of the classic trips in North America. (Note: Descending on skis from Lake Colden and Flowed Lands to Upper Works is a bit more difficult overall than descending from Lake Colden through Avalanche Pass to South Meadow. On a point-to-point trip between Upper Works and South Meadow, or vice versa, leaders may want to have those with lesser downhill skiing ability start at Upper Works.)

▶ The start to the Flowed Lands trip is at the end of a long, lonely road running from NY 28N near Newcomb past the nearly abandoned titanium mine at Tahawus to a collection of abandoned 19th-century buildings known variously as the Village of Adirondac or Upper Works. This road, posted as Blueridge Rd. and Co. Rt. 84 and marked with a DEC sign for the High Peaks, leaves NY 28N 7.3 mi northwest of Aiden Lair or about five miles east of the town hall in Newcomb. At 1.6 mi from NY 28N bear left onto Tahawus Rd. (Co. Rt. 28). At 6.0 mi from Rt. 28N, again bear left onto a narrower road marked with a sign for "Mt. Marcy and the High Peaks." Upper Works is 9.5 mi from NY 28N. An alternate approach is via Blue Ridge Road (now Co. Rt. 84) from North Hudson at Exit 29 on the Adirondack Northway. Drive 18.0 mi west from Exit 29 and turn right on the road to Tahawus. (This intersection is 1.6 mi north of NY 28N.) ◀

From the register at Upper Works (0.0 mi) the red- and yellow-marked trail proceeds nearly on the level to a junction at 0.4 mi. (The yellow-marked trail straight ahead leads to Indian Pass and Duck Hole.) Turning right and now following red markers, one soon reaches an extensive clearing with a view of Mount Colden. This clearing resulted from salvage logging in the aftermath of Hurricane Floyd, which struck the area in September 1999. After a few moderate ups and downs through this clearing, the trail descends to a beaver pond on a section of new (2011) trail that eliminates the two crossings of Calamity Brook. The new trail is wide and smooth except for 120 yd of rough going before joining the blue-marked trail from Indian Pass. This is the end of the red markers. Turning right and now following blue markers, the trail leads at first along the brook but soon begins a steady climb as it pulls away from the brook. At 2.3 mi, one rounds a sharp switchback to the right—for skiers the most challenging part of the descent. A few hundred yards above this switchback the grade eases, but one continues a gradual ascent to a crossing of Calamity Brook at 2.9 mi.

At this crossing there is a suspension bridge just upstream, but under most conditions one can cross the brook on the ice below the bridge. After crossing the brook, the steady climb resumes. At 3.3 mi the grade eases, followed by a series of short climbs and short, sharp descents. At 4.3 mi the trail reaches the north end of Calamity Pond, where a short side trail to the left leads to the large stone monument placed here in memory of David Henderson. Henderson was the driving force in developing the nineteenth century iron-mining operation at

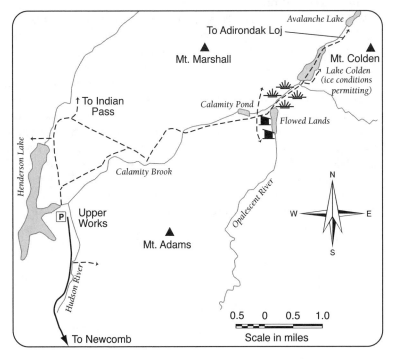

Flowed Lands and Lake Colden from Upper Works (Trip 12)

Tahawus. In 1848 he was accidentally shot at this spot while scouting the possibility of constructing a dam at Flowed Lands. The purpose of this dam would have been to divert the waters of the Opalescent River down Calamity Brook to increase the waterpower available to the then-proposed forge at Upper Works.

From the north end of Calamity Pond, the trail swings right and climbs gradually to Calamity Lean-tos on

TONY GOODWIN

Morgan Goodwin at Calamity Monument

the south side of Flowed Lands at 4.7 mi. The dam that once created this large lake was breached in 1981, but the open area remains and provides fine views of Mount Colden and the MacIntyre Range.

The hiking trail to Lake Colden around the west side of Flowed Lands is very rough, so most winter users continue straight ahead and down into the open area. After finding a location for crossing the channel of the Opalescent River, turn north and proceed to the upper end of the open area at approximately 5.3 mi. The trail to Lake Colden is just to the right of the Opalescent River. The trail leads immediately past a lean-to on the left and then past a lean-to on the right in another 100 yd. At 5.5 mi the trail comes to the bank of the Opalescent River at a point just above the confluence of the Opalescent and the outlet to Lake Colden. One now crosses the river and reaches the dam and bridge at Lake Colden at 5.6 mi.

Northern Region

Compared to the High Peaks region, this region sees less winter traffic on the trails, but that is not for lack of opportunities. The trips described below are only a few of the many possibilities. The terrain in the northern region is generally flatter than other parts of the Adirondacks, but the multitude of lakes, rivers, and open wetlands offer their share of views, especially when one can continue all the way to the middle to enjoy the full panorama. Snowfall amounts vary widely, with the Cranberry Lake, Tupper Lake, and Paul Smiths areas often having bountiful snow even when Plattsburgh and the St. Lawrence valley have bare ground.

There are no commercial cross-country ski centers in this region, although the Adirondack Park Visitor Interpretive Center in Paul Smiths (the "VIC," as it is often known) has approximately nine miles (fifteen kilometers) of trail with loops for all abilities. The VIC does groom these loops on a limited basis, but there are no rentals or lessons available. The VIC also offers parking, warming, and restroom facilities along with interpretive displays on the Adirondacks. As of 2012, there is a trail fee, and snowshoes are available for borrowing. The VIC is also the northern end of a 9.0 mi section of the Jackrabbit Trail that leads south to Lake Clear Junction. Check at the VIC for a map and conditions, and see Trip 4 in this guide for more details about the Jackrabbit Trail.

The VIC is open seven days a week, excepting Thanksgiving and Christmas. For information on VIC programs or for snow conditions in the area, the number is 518-327-3000. For snow conditions in the Tupper Lake area, call the Tupper Lake Chamber of Commerce at 518-359-3328.

Northern Region

Trail Ratings for Skiers

Beginner
18. Burn Road
    to Bum Pond
21. High Rock on
    the Oswegatchie River

Novice
15. Hays Brook
    Truck Trail
    and the
    "Sheep
    Meadow"

17. Lake Lila and
    Frederica Mountain
    (from trailhead to Lake Lila;
    see *Intermediate* entry below)

Novice-Intermediate
14. DeBar Game Management Area

Intermediate
13. St. Regis Canoe Area
16. Old Wawbeek Road–Deer Pond
    Loop
17. Lake Lila and Frederica Mountain
    (from Lake Lila to Frederica
    Mountain; see *Novice*
    entry above)
22. Peavine Swamp Trail
23. High Falls of the Oswegatchie
    River and Cat Mountain

Expert
19. Mt. Arab
20. St. Regis Mountain

Trail Ratings for Snowshoers

Beginner
14. DeBar Game Management
    Area
15. Hays Brook Truck Trail
    and the "Sheep Meadow"
18. Burn Road to Bum Pond
21. High Rock on the
    Oswegatchie River

Novice
13. St. Regis Canoe Area
16. Old Wawbeek Road–
    Deer Pond Loop
17. Lake Lila and
    Frederica Mountain
19. Mt. Arab
22. Peavine Swamp Trail

Intermediate
20. St. Regis Mountain
23. High Falls of the
    Oswegatchie River and
    Cat Mountain

13. St. Regis Canoe Area

Distance: 11.6 mi (18.7 km) round-trip to Fish Pond; 6.5 mi (10.5 km) loop trip to St. Regis and Little Clear Ponds
Difficulty: Ski, intermediate; snowshoe, novice
Maps: ADK Northern Region; USGS St. Regis Mountain and Upper Saranac Lake metric series

Owing to reliable snow, a variety of possible trips, and an absence of snowmobiles, this area sees more ski and snowshoe use than any other in the Northern Region. For winter users, the St. Regis Canoe Area offers a graded truck trail to Fish Pond with numerous variations using the lakes and portages connecting them. When the weather is fair and surface conditions suitable, most people prefer part of their trip to be on an open lake; but if this is not the case the truck trail offers excellent skiing or snowshoeing.

▶ The start is just off NY 30 on the side road that runs through the Adirondack Fish Hatchery. This road is 11.3 mi north of the junction of NY 30 and NY 3, or 2.3 mi south of the junction of NY 30 and NY 186.

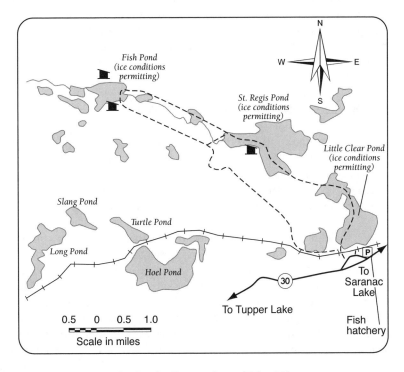

St. Regis Canoe Area (Trip 13)

A DEC sign just west of the hatchery marks the summer trailhead, but winter parking is at the end of Station St., which is just east of the summer trailhead. ◀

Begin by proceeding 200 yd along the railroad tracks. The truck trail then parallels the tracks for 0.7 mi before turning right and down to the gate and register at 0.9 mi. At first mostly on the level, the truck trail begins climbing gently at 2.1 mi, levels off and then climbs moderately to a crest at 2.7 mi. The descent leads to a junction at 3.3 mi with a road leading right to St. Regis Pond.

(To do the 6.5 mi loop trip, turn right, follow the road 0.2 mi to the small dam on St. Regis Pond, and then go to the far southeast corner to find the portage trail. Marked with a white sign, this trail leads 0.5 mi to Little Clear Pond. Complete the loop by proceeding generally along the right shore, around a point, and on to the boat-launch site at the south end of the pond. From here a short climb leads to the starting point.)

Continuing on the truck trail toward Fish Pond, an unmarked trail to Grass Pond diverges left at 3.5 mi, and a portage to Ochre Pond goes right at 3 .7 mi. After several more short climbs and descents, the truck trail reaches the southeast shore of Fish Pond at 5.8 mi. One lean-to is located about one-third of the way along the south shore; a second is located midway on the north shore. The usual return is via the truck trail, but a more difficult return of similar length is possible by following the series of portages to Mud, Ochre, and St. Regis Ponds.

14. DeBar Game Management Area

Distances: 3.0 mi (4.8 km) round-trip County Route 26 to Game Management Area; 8.0 mi (12.9 km) loop to Beaver Valley; 10.2 mi (16.5 km) point-to-point County Route 26 to Meacham Lake
Difficulty: Ski, novice-intermediate; snowshoe, beginner
Maps: USGS Debar Mountain and Meacham Lake 7.5' sheets

Characterized by relatively flat terrain, this remote area offers a number of interesting possibilities and is often blessed with snow when nearby areas are bare. Because all of the trips described here are on old roads, this area is skiable with a minimum of snow cover. The VIC at Paul Smiths is the closest place to call for conditions. There is currently no active game management in this area, but the roads are the legacy of an effort in the 1930s to propagate many species of plants and wildlife, including elk. Along the way, one will notice several pine plantations

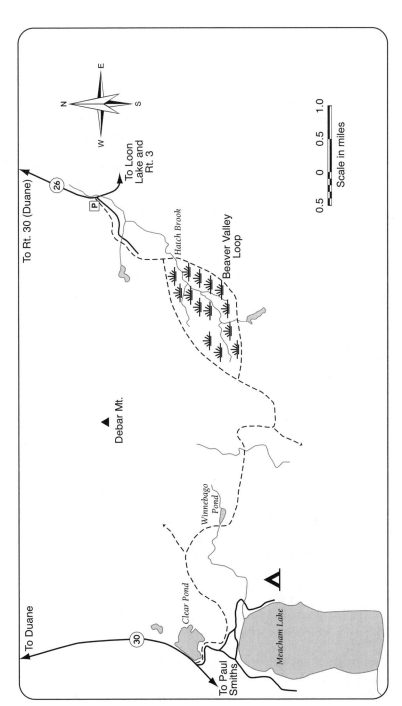

DeBar Game Management Area (Trip 14)

along with occasional sections of old wire fencing that was used to contain the nascent elk herd.

The route to Meacham Lake is now designated on regional snowmobile maps as a groomed snowmobile trail. As a result, traffic in this area has increased from what it was a few years ago, but snowmobile use usually isn't heavy enough to ruin one's day. Owing to the snowmobile traffic, however, the Beaver Valley Loop is recommended because much of that loop rarely has snowmobile traffic. In recent years there also has been some logging activity that has resulted in the first 1.4 mi of this tour being plowed, but not sanded. Public access is still permitted, and on most days it is still possible (if not ideal) to ski on the road until the tour enters state land at 1.5 mi.

▶ The start is the crossing of Hatch Brook on the remote and twisting Franklin County Route 26 (formerly NY 99), 10.9 mi northwest from NY 3, or 9.0 mi southeast of NY 30 at Duane. (The Meacham Lake end is on NY 30, 5.7 mi south of Duane or 3.0 mi north of the junction with NY 458.) ◀

The trip starts on an unplowed road (0.0 mi), which leads to a large open field at 1.5 mi. The views from this field are spectacular, particularly looking north to Baldface Mountain, and it makes a destination in itself. To continue, follow the road as it swings left and on to the south end of the field at 1.7 mi. Here there is a choice of three roads. The right and middle roads both lead to Meacham Lake, whereas the left road is the return from the Beaver Valley Loop as described below. The middle road has a bit of rough going at some washouts, but is less overgrown than the right-hand road. Those proceeding on the right or middle road will find that the two rejoin at 2.2 mi, where there is a barrier, then a beaver dam on the right, followed by a short climb. Now gently rolling, the road reaches a junction of two roads at 4.0 mi.

(The road straight ahead leads to Meacham Lake. Bear right at 5.5 mi where the Hays Brook Wetland Trail goes left. The road then swings to the west, climbs gently, and then descends past Winnebago Pond to a junction with the Debar Mountain Trail at 7.8 mi. From here the route is marked with standard red DEC markers to the Meacham Lake Campground at 9.0 mi, with the main campground road reached at 9.5 mi. In recent years the north entrance to this campground road has been plowed to facilitate ice fishing; if not plowed, it is another 0.7 mi to NY 30.)

Turning left at the junction, one soon crosses a dam that was one of several constructed in the 1930s as part of an effort to encourage wetland species, including beaver. After the dam, there are two short, steep climbs followed by a long plateau as the road swings left and heads back to the north. At the end of the plateau there are two gradual descents and a steeper, more "exciting" descent to a bridge over Hatch Brook, and then a short, gentle climb back up to complete the loop at the south end of the open meadow at 6.3 mi. From here, return through the meadow and back along the access road to NY 26 at 8.0 mi.

15. Hays Brook Truck Trail to Grass Pond and the "Sheep Meadow"

Distances: 7.8 mi (12.6 km) round-trip to the Sheep Meadow; 3.8 mi (6.1 km) round-trip to Grass Pond
Difficulty: Ski, novice; snowshoe, beginner
Maps: Page 66. ADK Northern Region (partial; St. Regis only); USGS St. Regis metric series and Meacham Lake 7.5' sheet

Both destinations described here offer not only easy terrain and a scenic lean-to but also usually bountiful snow. The longer route to the Sheep Meadow has a few short pitches that may be a bit challenging for novice skiers, but overall these wide roads offer easy travel.

▶ The start is at Mountain Pond at the end of a 0.2 mi access road off NY 30. Marked by a large DEC sign, this access road is 3.8 mi north of the junction of NY 86 in Paul Smiths, and 5.4 mi south of the junction of NY 458. From the parking area at the end of the plowed road, continue another 150 yd to the barrier gate and register. There are both horse and snowmobile markers on the trail, but snowmobiles are rarely encountered. ◀

Following the truck trail north from the gate (0.0 mi), one crosses the Osgood River at 0.5 mi with the junction of the trail to Grass Pond just beyond.

(The trail to Grass Pond makes a short, moderate climb to the top of a high bank above the Osgood River, after which it is mostly flat to the lean-to at Grass Pond at 1.9 mi. One road leads left from the lean-to, down to the outlet, and on to a former lean-to site on the north shore. Another road going past the lean-to can be skied partway along the east shore, but soon becomes overgrown. The surface of the pond does not offer additional views, but it may offer some sun to make it a warmer lunch spot than the lean-to.)

Just beyond the side trail to Grass Pond, the marked route to the Sheep Meadow diverges to the left to "cut the corner" and save 0.3 mi.

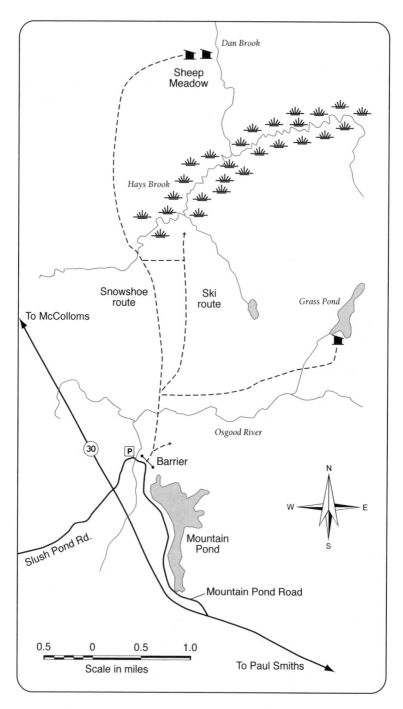

Hays Brook Truck Trail and the "Sheep Meadow" (Trip 15)

Those on snowshoes may choose to follow the marked route, but the easiest skiing is found by staying on the truck trail, which climbs for another 0.2 mi and is then flat to a junction at 1.2 mi. Turn left here. The trail continues flat, but begins to descend at 1.5 mi and rejoins the marked route at 1.6 mi, after which it continues to descend to a bridge over Hays Brook at 1.8 mi. After the bridge, the trail climbs a short pitch, and levels out at 2.1 mi. It is then mostly level to the lean-tos at 3.9 mi.

16. Old Wawbeek Road–Deer Pond Loop

Distance: 7.3 mi (11.8 km) loop
Difficulty: Ski, intermediate; snowshoe, novice
Maps: ADK Northern Region (partial; Upper Saranac Lake only); USGS Tupper Lake and Upper Saranac Lake metric series

Around 1985 the DEC designated these trails for cross-country skiing, a change from their previous designation as snowmobile trails. There is still some snowmobile traffic on the Old Wawbeek Road, but the trails to Deer Pond usually are used only by skiers and snowshoers. Deer Pond itself is a beautiful destination, although the trails there are a bit rough and steep in a few spots. The Old Wawbeek Road, the predecessor to the present NY 3, offers a total of about four miles of novice skiing through an interesting variety of forests.

▶ The start, 0.8 mi west of the junction of NY 3 and NY 30 (known as Wawbeek Corners), is marked by a sign for Saranac Lakes Wild Forest Cross-Country Ski Trails. One can also start at Bull Point on NY 30, 1.7 mi north of Wawbeek Corners across the highway from a sign for "Bungalow Bay—Private Drive." The skiing is generally easier if the loop is done counterclockwise. ◀

From the southern parking lot (0.0 mi), bear right and follow yellow ski disks along the Old Wawbeek Road for 1.2 mi to a junction with a red-marked DEC trail. (This trail leads 0.7 mi to the alternate start on Rt. 30 at Bull Point.) Turning left at this junction, the trail remains mostly level to a spruce-fir swamp, after which it begins to climb at 2.1 mi. The climb is moderate to steep at times as the trail traverses under a line of cliffs up to the right. At 2.9 mi the trail reaches a junction on a ridgetop overlooking Deer Pond. The trail right goes to Lead Pond. Bearing left at this junction, the trail descends to the south end of Deer Pond at 3.2 mi.

From the south end of Deer Pond the trail swings left and up for 300 yd through mature hardwoods to the top of a ridge, followed by a gen-

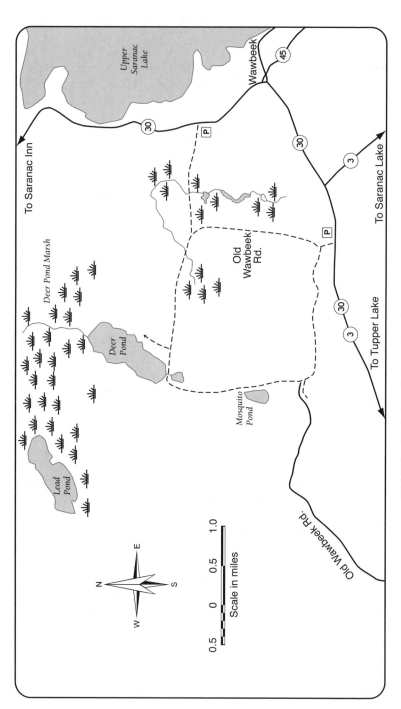

Old Wawbeek Road–Deer Pond Loop (Trip 16)

tle to moderate descent to Mosquito Pond at 3.9 mi. After another brief climb, the trail descends to cross the outlet to a beaver pond at 4.4 mi. Again climbing, one comes to a split with ski trail markers going left but a more obvious trail going right. The marked ski route was apparently intended to avoid a very steep little pitch on the original snowmobile trail, but in any event the two routes rejoin in 200 yd and continue through a plantation of Norway spruce, a favorite deer wintering area, before reaching the Old Wawbeek Road at 4.8 mi. Turn left and follow the road back to the starting point at 7.3 mi.

17. Lake Lila and Frederica Mountain

Distance: 15.0 mi (24.2 km) round-trip to Lake Lila, 18.0 mi (29.0 km) round-trip to Frederica Mountain via Lake Lila
Elevation change: 535 ft (163 m)
Summit elevation: 2240 ft (683 m)
Difficulty: Ski, novice to Lake Lila, intermediate to Frederica Mountain; snowshoe, novice
Maps: Page 71. USGS Little Tupper Lake, Beaver River, and Forked Lake metric series, and Wolf Mountain 7.5' sheet

I once described Lake Lila as "a near perfect destination for a ski tour with less-than-perfect means of access on skis." The negative part of this statement applies less today because the summer access road sees much less logging during the winter. One may still have to use the alternate approach, however.

▶ Both approaches start on the Sabattis road, which has two branches that leave NY 30 11.5 mi south of the village of Tupper Lake and 7.0 mi north of Long Lake, respectively. Via either approach it is approximately three miles to the junction of the two branches of Sabattis Road at the northeast end of Little Tupper Lake and then 4.7 mi farther west to Lake Lila Road, the preferred access, on the left. If not plowed owing to logging operations, park on Sabattis Road and proceed gently up and down for 5.8 mi to a summer parking lot and barrier gate. From here, a trail leads 0.3 mi to the north shore of Lake Lila. If ice conditions are questionable, however, continue on the road around the west shore of the lake to a junction with a road at 8.4 mi leading up to the Nehasane station on the abandoned railroad.

[The alternate approach is via the abandoned Adirondack Railway line from the end of the road at Sabattis, another 3.3 mi beyond. This route

sees heavy snowmobile traffic and is best done on a weekday. Ski south
on the railroad to Nehasane station, located just past milepost 88, and
then to the shore of Lake Lila 7.5 mi from Sabattis. (The "H" on each
milepost indicates distance from Herkimer, the original southern termi-
nus of the line.)] ◄

Whether proceeding across the lake or approaching via the road or
railroad, the most scenic point is the large clearing on the southwest
shore where William Seward Webb's Nehasane Lodge once stood.
Constructed in 1892 when Webb's Mohawk and Malone Railroad (the
early name for the present Adirondack Railroad) was also completed,
this imposing structure was torn down in the early 1980s after the state
purchased this property.

The side trip to Frederica Mountain begins 0.2 mi west (towards the
railroad) and is marked with yellow markers. It follows a road that goes
south, turns west and climbs to cross the tracks in 0.5 mi, and then continues to climb in stages to a junction at 1.0 mi. Here the trail to
Frederica Mountain goes right and climbs steadily to the summit, 1.5 mi
from Lake Lila. The summit offers extensive views to the east and south,
including the High Peaks nearly fifty miles distant.

18. Burn Road to Bum Pond

Distance: 10.0 mi (16.1 km) round-trip
Difficulty: Ski, beginner; snowshoe, beginner
Maps: DEC William C. Whitney Wilderness brochure; USGS Little
Tupper Lake metric series

The State's acquisition of the William C. Whitney Area in 1998 has
opened up several excellent new opportunities for winter trips.
Described below is just one of the shorter possibilities.

This area offers many destinations for skiers and snowshoers of all
abilities via the many wide lumber roads built before the state acquired
the property. This part of the Adirondacks generally receives abundant
snowfall, while the smooth roads make Whitney Area trips good choic-
es in low-snow conditions. Trips in this area will be included in the new
edition of ADK's *Guide to Adirondack Trails: Northern Region* due out in
Autumn 2004. For now, this description and the DEC brochure suffice
to introduce hikers and skiers to this relatively new property. (The
brochure may be obtained from ADK's Lake George facility or from the
DEC.) Additionally, the registration stations at both the Burn Road and

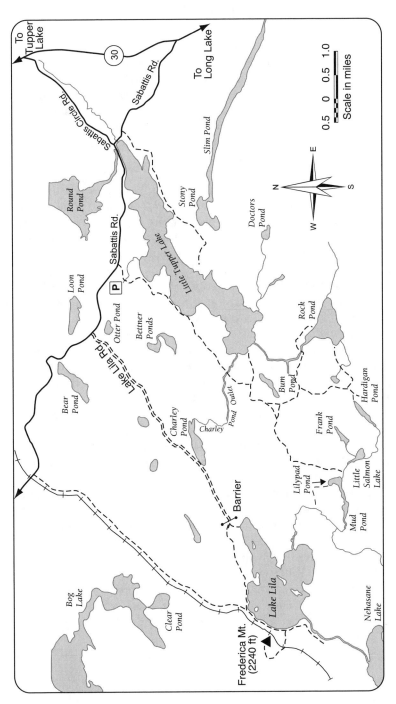

Lake Lila and Frederica Mountain (Trip 17) and Burn Road to Burn Pond (Trip 18)

Stony Pond Road trailheads have maps of the area posted with existing trails clearly marked. The Stony Pond Road is another good possibility and offers terrain similar to that traversed by the Burn Road.

▶ Access to the Burn Road is on Sabattis Road, which has two branches that leave NY 30 11.5 mi south of Tupper Lake and 7.0 mi north of Long Lake, respectively. Via either approach it is approximately three miles to the junction of the two branches of Sabattis Road at the northeast end of Little Tupper Lake and then 2.9 mi. farther west to the trailhead on the left. ◀

Bum Pond is the first small pond that can be reached via the Burn Road, one of several wide gravel roads in the William C. Whitney Area that are now foot trails. Other destinations for the more ambitious include Lilypad and Hardigan Ponds (16.4 mi round-trip) and Rock Pond (17.0 mi round-trip). For the less ambitious, there are many locations in the first 2.0 mi from which one can access the shore of Little Tupper Lake, and the hilltop and open area at the crossing of Charley Pond Outlet makes an attractive destination for an 8.0 mi round-trip. Signs also refer to "Old Frenchman's Mine" on the route to Rock and Hardigan Ponds, but in reality this is nothing more than a restored gravel pit, one that presumably had been used by some of the French-Canadian lumbermen to build the extensive network of gravel roads.

From the gate (0.0 mi), the road descends gently, crosses the outlet to Otter Pond, and then continues on the flat. After nearing the shore of Little Tupper Lake at 1.0 mi, the road climbs slightly and descends to the lake again. As of 2001 there was a sign with a large "2" here indicating two miles (plus additional signs for three, four, and five miles farther on.) From here the road is close to the lake for another 0.5 mi, after which it begins a gradual climb.

Bear right at an unmarked junction in a gravel pit and continue to climb to a junction at the top of the grade at 2.9 mi. Turn left and continue to climb slightly to a hilltop, followed by a gentle descent to Charley Pond Outlet at just over 4.0 mi. Past the outlet, the road climbs through an open area to a junction at 4.7 mi. The road to the right leads to Hardigan, Lily Pad, and Rock Ponds. Turning left, follow the road past a bog on the right to a rough trail down to the north end of Bum Pond at 5.0 mi. The road continues to Camp Bliss, a former private camp and now a designated campsite at the southwest end of Little Tupper Lake.

19. Mt. Arab

Distance: 2.0 mi (3.2 km) round-trip
Elevation change: 760 ft (232 m)
Summit elevation: 2545 ft (776 m)
Difficulty: Snowshoe, novice; ski, expert
Map: USGS Piercefield metric series

Mt. Arab is a wonderful little gem tucked away in a remote part of the
Adirondacks. The fire tower was restored in 1999 and is now safe to
climb, although views can be obtained, especially in winter, without
climbing the tower. Views range from some of the High Peaks to the east
to vast expanses without structures to the north and west. The trail may

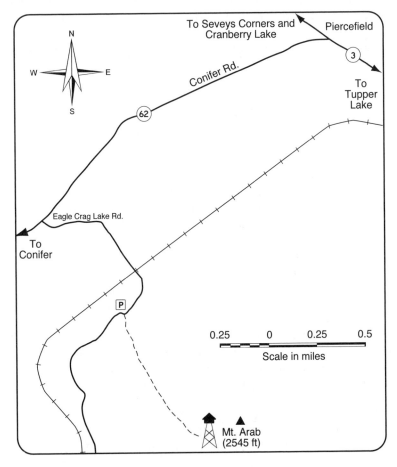

Mt. Arab (Trip 19)

be a bit too steep in spots for a novice snowshoe rating, but its short distance makes this a trip for almost any snowshoer and a good chance to practice climbing steeper slopes. The trail is definitely not ski terrain, but open woods along much of the trail permit expert skiers to descend the mountain under good snow conditions.

▶ The start is off Conifer Road (County Route 62), which intersects NY 3 at 7.0 mi. west of the junction of NY 3 and NY 30 in Tupper Lake Village and 10.4 mi. east of the intersection with NY 56 at Seveys Corners. Follow the Conifer Road 1.8 mi. south to Eagle Crag Lake Road on the left. Follow this road 0.9 mi. to the trailhead on the left. There is parking on the right, opposite the trailhead. ◀

From the trailhead (0.0 mi), the trail quickly begins to climb through open hardwoods. It maintains a steady grade before easing off at 0.8 mi. amidst some large rock outcrops. About one hundred feet to the right is an overlook of the hamlet of Conifer along with Mt. Arab and Eagle Crag Lakes. The trail then begins to circle and finally reaches the summit at 1.0 mi.

20. St. Regis Mountain

Distance: 6.8 mi (11.0 km) round-trip
Elevation change: 1265 ft (386 m)
Summit elevation: 2874 ft (876 m)
Difficulty: Snowshoe, intermediate; ski, expert
Maps: ADK Northern Region; USGS St. Regis Mountain metric series

With its bald summit and sweeping views, St. Regis Mountain is a popular destination in both summer and winter. The upper sections of this trail are just steep enough that it is recommended as a snowshoe hike, but the open woods next to the trail give skilled skiers many possibilities for an interesting, if challenging, descent.

▶ The start for the trail has been relocated to keep it off the private property of Camp Topridge. The start is on Keese Mills Road, which begins 200 yd north of the intersection of NY 30 and NY 86 in Paul Smiths. Proceed 2.6 mi along Keese Mills Road to a parking lot at left just beyond the gravel road leading to Camp Topridge. Park in the lot or, if not plowed, on Keese Mills Road. Do not park on the entrance road. ◀

From the parking lot (0.0 mi) proceed down the Topridge Road for 0.1 mi to the trail on the right. The trail ascends gradually to moderately to a height of land at 1.0 mi in an impressive stand of hemlocks. The trail

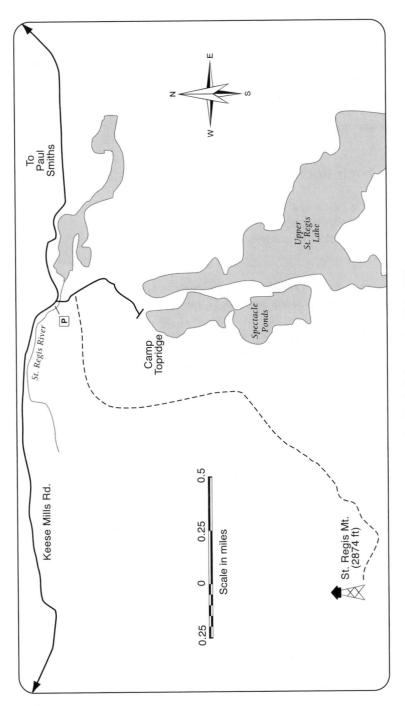

St. Regis Mountain (Trip 20)

then descends to a low point at 1.5 mi followed by a gradual to moderate climb to the junction with the old trail and a bridge across a stream at 2.2 mi. From this point the trail steepens, passing enormous boulders at 3.2 mi before reaching the summit at 3.4 mi. Although it has been scheduled for removal several times already, the abandoned fire tower is still standing (2002).

21. High Rock on the Oswegatchie River

Distance: 7.6 mi (12.3 km) round-trip
Difficulty: Ski, beginner; snowshoe, beginner
Maps: ADK Northern Region; USGS Newton Falls and Five Ponds 7.5' sheets

This trip, with very gentle grades, follows an old truck trail that was originally built as a logging railroad. Following the "microburst" storm of 1995, the trail system in this area was altered considerably, with some very heavily damaged trails abandoned altogether. This trip is the first part of what *Guide to Adirondack Trails: Northern Region* describes as the High Falls Loop, but the approach via Dead Creek Flow described below is a shorter route than *Northern Region's* approach to High Falls. As described below, this trip makes High Rock the focal point because it is a destination worth visiting all on its own, and the gentle terrain makes this a perfect introductory trip for skiers or snowshoers.

The Rich Lumber Company built the railroad that created these gentle grades and operated it from 1902 to 1910. As was the practice at the time, the company cut nearly every marketable tree and would have continued had not fires burned some of the available timber. While the timber was in good supply, however, the now sleepy little village of Wanakena was a bustling hub with five large mills and all of the homes, boarding houses, and stores to support the labor force needed to cut and mill the timber. All of the mills were located south of the river along the beginning of this route, although little sign remains of this extensive industrial development.

▶ To reach Wanakena, turn off NY 3 at a point 8.0 mi west of Cranberry Lake or 6.0 mi east of Star Lake. Proceed south on the road for 0.8 mi and bear right across a bridge over the Oswegatchie River. The start is just beyond on the right. ◀

From the gate, the trail is flat as it passes an old mill pond on the left at 0.2 mi and then crosses Skate Creek on a culvert at 0.7 mi. Shortly

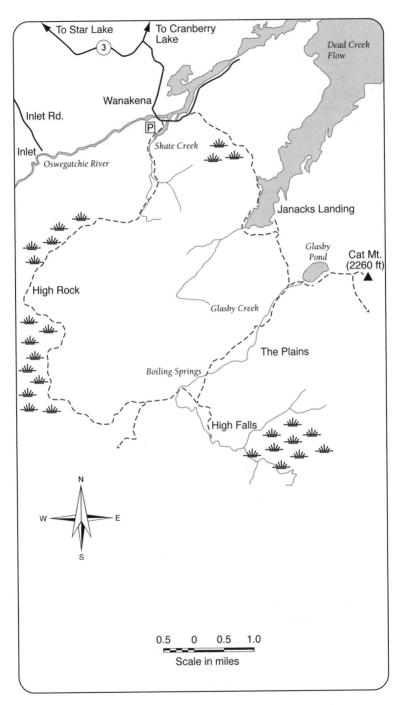

High Rock on the Oswegatchie River (Trip 21)
and High Falls and Cat Mountain (Trip 23)

after this crossing, the trail begins a gentle climb to the junction with the now-abandoned Leary Trail at 1.8 mi. (Once a shorter route to High Falls, this was abandoned owing to extensive storm damage.)

Past this point, the trail continues to climb gently for another 300 yd. The narrow cuts through the blowdown indicate the severity of the 1995 storm. At 2.0 mi the trail begins a gentle descent to a partially open marsh on the right, followed by a climb to a height of land at 3.5 mi. After another short descent and climb, the trail reaches an unmarked side trail to High Rock at 3.7 mi. The side trail proceeds about two hundred yards to an open area with the best views up and to the right.

22. Peavine Swamp Trail

Distance: 8.2 mi (13.2 km) round-trip
Difficulty: Ski, intermediate; snowshoe, novice
Maps: ADK Northern Region; USGS Cranberry Lake and Newton Falls 7.5′ sheets

Constructed as a ski trail in the early 1990s, this trail has not received as much use as was anticipated and the two side loops are rarely used, perhaps in part because they are not well marked. Nevertheless, the trip to the lean-to and back does see steady use throughout the winter. This means that although one may have to break trail, one is likely to be breaking out only the most recent storm and not an entire winter's accumulation. A further attraction of this trail is that it often has snow even when areas close by, but a bit lower, don't. And as a designated ski trail, snowmobiles are prohibited.

In general, the trail runs from NY 3 along the edge of an extensive swamp before climbing a low ridge and ending at a secluded lean-to on Inlet Flow, one of the many long narrow bays radiating from the main body of Cranberry Lake. The lean-to site is scenic, and the "up and over" nature of the trail means that one has interesting terrain in both directions.

▶ The trail begins 1.2 mi west of the bridge over the Oswegatchie River at the outskirts of Cranberry Lake village. ◀

The trail is flat for 0.3 mi to a junction (unmarked as of 2002) with the Balanced Rock Loop, which diverges left. The trail then climbs to some undulating terrain with the Balanced Rock Loop coming in on the left at 1.0 mi. The trail now descends gently to a small stream with the Christmas Tree Loop (also unmarked), diverging left just before crossing

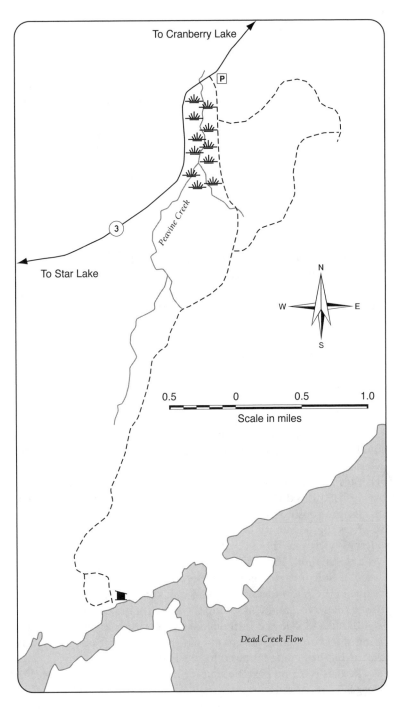

To Cranberry Lake

P

3

To Star Lake

Peavine Creek

N
W — E
S

0.5   0   0.5   1.0
Scale in miles

Dead Creek Flow

Peavine Swamp Trail (Trip 22)

the stream. The trail then climbs gradually with a moderate climb starting at 1.6 mi. Along this climb, look for two very large spruce trees that
somehow survived the logging, and then just past a small stream at 2.0
mi look for two hemlocks that DEC foresters have measured at 40 inches and 42 inches diameter at breast height.

The trail then makes its steepest climb to a high point at 2.6 mi, after
which it makes a gradual descent with the Christmas Tree Loop coming
in from the left at 2.8 mi. The trail descends a bit more, then rises to a
height of land at 3.0 mi. Now following an old road, the trail descends
to a junction at 3.8 mi. The left fork offers the easiest descent to the lean-
to at 4.1 mi.

23. High Falls of the Oswegatchie River and Cat Mountain

Distance: 14.0 mi (22.6 km) round-trip to High Falls; 11.2 mi (18.1 km)
    to Cat Mountain
Elevation change: 760 ft (232 m)
Summit elevation: 2260 ft (689 m)
Difficulty: Ski, intermediate; snowshoe, intermediate
Maps: Page 77. ADK Northern Region; USGS Five Ponds and
    Newton Falls, 7.5′ sheets

Although this trip has seen some winter traffic in recent years, one
should assume that trail breaking will usually be necessary, at least
beyond Dead Creek Flow. As originally described, this trip approached
High Falls via the truck trail and the Leary Trail. With the Leary Trail
now closed, this is the shortest route to High Falls, although there is one
steep section south of Janacks Landing. For the adventurous, this route
also offers the possibility of a trip to Cat Mountain and its "ultimate"
wilderness view—i.e. a pond, a low ridge, and miles of trees.

As a destination, High Falls can perhaps be summed up as a remote
gateway to still greater remoteness. Beyond High Falls is the largest trail-
less area in the Adirondacks, a seldom visited region stretching south to
Stillwater Reservoir and containing the largest stand of virgin timber in
the Adirondacks. See the introduction to the High Rock trip for both
driving directions and background on the lumbering operations that
built the railroad grade followed for the first 3.0 mi of the trip.

▶ The start is 0.5 mi past the start for High Rock on the right. See Trip
21, page 76. ◀

From the trail register (0.0 mi) the trail is nearly flat to a beaver pond at 1.0 mi. There is a reroute to the right, but winter travelers should be able to cross the pond and continue on the flat to the beginning of a gentle descent at 1.2 mi that leads to the edge of Dead Creek Flow at 1.5 mi. The trail now follows the shore to a junction with a trail to the lean-to at Janacks Landing at 2.9 mi; but if ice conditions permit, a ski straight across the flow to the lean-to and along the side trail will save approximately 0.5 mi. From this junction, the

St. Regis Mountain trail

trail soon begins to climb moderately, with a few steeper pitches, to Sand Hill Junction at 4.0 mi where the trip to Cat Mountain diverges.

(To ascend Cat Mountain, turn left and follow the Cowhorn Junction Trail up moderately to a waterfall at the outlet to Glasby Pond and then on gradually to the junction with the Cat Mountain trail at 0.9 mi. Turn left and up moderately for 0.3 mi to the base of some cliffs through which the trail ascends. These next few hundred yards are definitely not ski terrain and snowshoers are likely to have to kick a few steps, but they are a reasonable price to pay for a seldom visited view on an otherwise easy 11.0 mi of terrain. From the summit, one sees Cat Mountain Pond at the base, and Three Mile Mountain to the side, but otherwise the view is of unbroken woods with not a trace of civilization to be seen.)

Continuing on toward High Falls, the trail descends moderately along Glasby Creek to a crossing at 4.2 mi and then is nearly straight and level along the base of Three Mile Mountain to a junction near the Oswegatchie River at 6.6 mi. This is the continuation of the trail via High Rock. Turning left, High Falls is reached at 7.0 mi.

Central Region

There are enough possibilities for cross-country skiing and snowshoeing in this region that the eleven trips described are but a small sampling of its winter opportunities. The region's centerpiece is the Siamese Ponds Wilderness Area, in which there are both short wilderness jaunts and long, rugged wilderness treks, but the outlying areas also offer a tremendous variety of destinations and terrain. Snowfall is generally plentiful in this region.

The only commercially developed cross-country ski centers are near North Creek. Garnet Hill Lodge is the most established operation, offering lodging as well as trails and direct access to several of the described tours. Cunningham's Ski Barn offers some interesting skiing near the Hudson River, while Gore Mountain maintains a few trails at the base of the downhill area. In addition to the commercial cross-country centers, the Visitor Interpretive Center in Newcomb has a few miles of snowshoe trails and can give information on snow cover in the northern part of this region. Finally, the villages of Speculator (permit required on some trails) and Indian Lake maintain small loop trails for cross-country skiing.

Central Region Cross-Country Ski Centers and Sites
Cunningham's Ski Barn 518-251-3215
Garnet Hill Lodge 518-251-2821
Gore Mountain Ski Center 518-251-2411
Indian Lake 518-648-5112
Speculator 518-548-5421
Visitor Interpretive Center at Newcomb 518-582-2000

Central Region

Trail Ratings for Skiers

Novice
26. John Pond
30. Hoffman Notch
    (from trailhead to
    Big Marsh;
    see *Intermediate*
    entry below)
31. Cheney Pond and
    Lester Flow

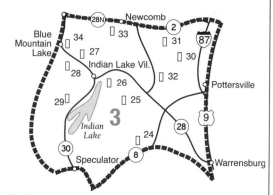

Novice-Intermediate
27. Tirrell Pond from the South
    via Northville-Placid Trail

Intermediate
24. East Branch Sacandaga River Trail
25. Puffer Pond from Thirteenth Lake
28. Stephens and Cascade Ponds
30. Hoffman Notch (from Big Marsh to
    Hoffman Notch; see *Novice* entry above)
32. Stony Pond

Intermediate-Expert
33. Goodnow Mountain

Expert
29. Snowy Mountain
34. Blue Mountain

Trail Ratings for Snowshoers

Beginner
26. John Pond
27. Tirrell Pond from the South
    via Northville-Placid Trail
31. Cheney Pond and Lester Flow

Novice
24. East Branch Sacandaga River Trail
25. Puffer Pond from Thirteenth Lake
28. Stephens and Cascade Ponds
30. Hoffman Notch (from trailhead

to Big Marsh; see *Intermediate*
entry below)
32. Stony Pond
33. Goodnow Mountain

Intermediate
29. Snowy Mountain
30. Hoffman Notch (from Big Marsh
    to Hoffman Notch;
    see *Novice* entry at left)
34. Blue Mountain

24. East Branch Sacandaga River Trail

Distance: 11.1 mi (19.9 km) point-to-point
Difficulty: Ski, intermediate; snowshoe, novice
Maps: Page 86. ADK Central Region; USGS Thirteenth Lake and Bakers
Mills metric series

This challenging trip is one of the classic wilderness traverses in the Adirondacks. Many skiers will elect to start at the south end because it is easier to ascend the steep section next to NY 8 than to descend this 0.3 mi on tired legs at the end of the trip. It is, however, definitely possible to ski down this section should the group desire to split up and arrange for an exchange of car keys in the middle. One advantage in skiing from north to south is that much of the first ten miles is gently downhill rather than the other way around. For snowshoers this hill shouldn't be a problem either way. The logistics involved in shuttling cars make a "key-swap" plan attractive on this trip; but, as with any such arrangement, there should be two self-sufficient parties with contingency plans in the event of a failure to meet as planned.

▶ The north end of this trip begins at the end of Thirteenth Lake Road, which leaves NY 28 just north of North River. A DEC sign for the Siamese Ponds Wilderness Area marks this turn, along with signs for Garnet Hill Lodge. At 3.4 mi from NY 28, bear left at a junction and then bear right at the next two junctions to reach a fair-sized parking area at the end of the plowed road. (The groomed ski trails in this area are maintained by Garnet Hill Lodge and require a trail fee.) Continue straight ahead to the gate at the boundary of the Siamese Ponds Wilderness Area.

The south end of this trip is on NY 8, 4.0 mi west of Bakers Mills, at a large parking lot with a DEC sign. ◀

The trail begins with a steep climb of 240 ft to a col on the shoulder of Eleventh Mountain. Here the route of the old stage road enters from the left, and the trail follows this route all the way to Thirteenth Lake. From the col, the trail descends gently to Diamond Brook at 1.5 mi and then begins following the northeast bank of the river up to Burnt Shanty Clearing at 2.7 mi. At 3.5 mi one reaches a junction. (The trail at right is the route of the original road and trail. It misses the lean-to, but potentially offers easier skiing than the current marked route while also saving 0.3 mi.)

Turning left, the trail proceeds along the bank of the river for 0.5 mi to a lean-to and suspension bridge. (The bridge leads to the Siamese Ponds Trail.) The lean-to, which makes a scenic stopping point, is just to the right of the bridge. From the lean-to, the trail continues, with some

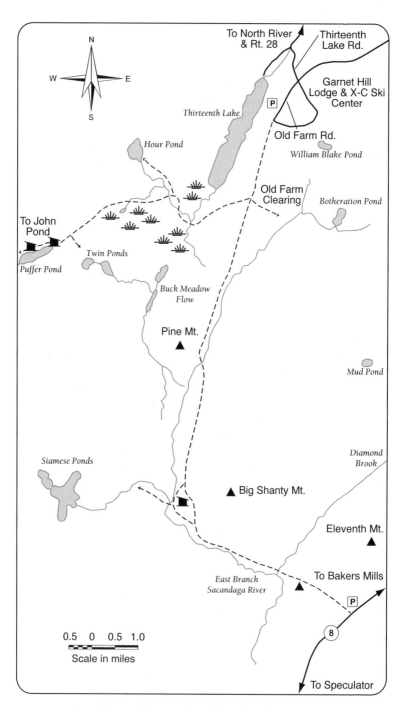

East Branch Sacandaga River Trail (Trip 24)
and Puffer Pond from Thirteenth Lake (Trip 25)

rough spots, along the bank of the river to the junction with the old trail at 4.3 mi. Bearing left, one reaches Big Shanty Flow at 4.6 mi.

Continuing on near the flow, there is a large boulder on the right at 5.2 mi, a bridge across Cross Brook at 5.7 mi, and the crossing of the East Branch on a bridge at 6.6 mi. At about seven miles there is a short climb followed by a level section and then two more distinctly steeper grades to a height of land at 8.9 mi. (With less than ideal snow, descending this section can be tricky owing to some large rocks on the eroded grades.) From the height of land a gradual descent leads to the junction with the Puffer Pond Trail at 9.5 mi, followed by Old Farm Clearing at 9.6 mi. From here, easy terrain leads to the plowed end of Thirteenth Lake Road at 11.1 mi.

25. Puffer Pond from Thirteenth Lake

Distance: 11.0 mi (17.7 km) round-trip
Difficulty: Ski, intermediate; snowshoe, novice
Maps: ADK Central Region; USGS Thirteenth Lake metric series

Set between the steep slopes of Bullhead and Puffer Mountains, Puffer Pond is an attractive destination, whether approached from Thirteenth Lake or Kings Flow (via Puffer Pond Brook Trail.) The Thirteenth Lake approach is generally the most popular, and gives one the option of a side trip to Hour Pond. Crossing Hour Pond Outlet is potentially a problem, but a relatively short and easy bushwhack can bypass the problem.

▶ The start is the same as the northern start for the East Branch of the Sacandaga Trail (see Trip 24). ◀

From the parking area (0.0 mi), proceed to the junction just beyond Old Farm Clearing at 1.6 mi. Turning right, the trail descends to cross an inlet to Thirteenth Lake at 2.5 mi. The trail then begins to climb, parallels Hour Pond Outlet, and then crosses this brook at 2.8 mi. (If this crossing is not possible, continue up the bank of the brook for 150 yd and then climb forty to fifty vertical feet to a higher shelf, which is followed for another 200 yd to a small brook. The Puffer Pond Trail is found just across this small brook.)

Assuming the crossing is feasible, at 2.9 mi the trail reaches the junction with a trail leading right 1.2 mi to Hour Pond—a charming destination in itself or a pleasant side trip. Continuing on, the Puffer Pond Trail recrosses Hour Pond Outlet and ascends rolling terrain to a crest at 3.6 mi, from which there is a good view of Puffer Mountain. After descending to an abandoned beaver dam and meadow at 3.7 mi, the trail climbs moderately for 150 yd, followed by mostly level terrain to Puffer Pond at 5.5 mi. There is one lean-to at the east end and another 0.2 mi along the north shore.

26. John Pond

Distance: 6.0 mi (9.7 km) round-trip
Difficulty: Ski, novice; snowshoe, beginner
Maps: ADK Central Region; USGS Thirteenth Lake metric series

Combining an attractive destination with easy but interesting terrain, this trip has become quite popular in recent years. One can also make this an 8.0 mi intermediate-level, point-to-point trip by starting at Kings Flow and proceeding via the Puffer Pond Trail and John Pond Crossover.

▶ The start for John Pond is southeast of the village of Indian Lake. From the intersection of NY 28 and NY 30 in Indian Lake, proceed south

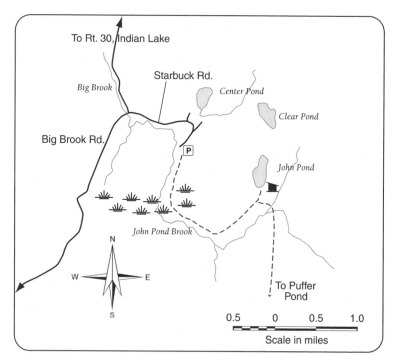

John Pond (Trip 26)

on NY 30 0.6 mi and turn left on Big Brook Road for 3.3 mi to Starbuck Road. Turn left for 0.4 mi and bear left at the entrance to Wilderness Lodge. Now on Lake View Drive, proceed 0.5 mi to a T intersection where one turns right 0.2 mi to the trailhead. There may be vehicle tracks for another 0.1 mi to the barrier, but the end of plowing is the best place to start. (Coming from the east on NY 28, one can also reach Big Brook Road by turning left on Chamberlain Road, County Route 18, at the top of a long hill, 1.0 mi west of the sign for the Indian Lake town line.) ◄

From the trailhead (0.0 mi), the trail is gently rolling for 0.7 mi to a fork where the John Pond Trail goes sharp left and continues to climb in generally easy stages. At 1.7 mi a side trail left leads to the burial ground of Peter Savary and Eliza Emilia King, two children who died of diphtheria. At 1.9 mi the John Pond Crossover Trail diverges to the right, after which the trail rises in several easy pitches to reach the lean-to at 2.3 mi.

27. Tirrell Pond from the South via Northville-Placid Trail

Distance: 7.0 mi (11.3 km) round-trip
Difficulty: Ski, novice-intermediate; snowshoe, beginner
Maps: Page 90. ADK Central Region; USGS Blue Mountain Lake and Deerland metric series

Long a favorite of winter campers because of its two lean-tos and wonderful scenery, Tirrell Pond has more recently become a favored destination for skiers as well.

▶ This trip follows the Northville-Placid Trail, which crosses NY 28 and NY 30 2.6 mi east of Blue Mountain Lake. The Tirrell Pond trip starts on the north side of the highway. ◄

From the trailhead (0.0 mi), the trail climbs diagonally up a road cut to a trail register and then heads north following blue markers. At 0.6 mi the trail bears left at a junction with a tote road and descends to cross two wet areas on good bridges. At 1.7 mi the trail bears left and up, crossing a lumber road and then a brook at 1.9 mi. Here it turns sharp left to follow the north bank of the brook. Recrossing the brook twice, the trail climbs away from the brook and crosses a lumber road at 2.5 mi. Now the grade eases as the trail passes through a clearing, crosses another brook, and reaches a second clearing at 2.8 mi. A right turn and then a left turn on good roads are followed by a recently cut area and then a

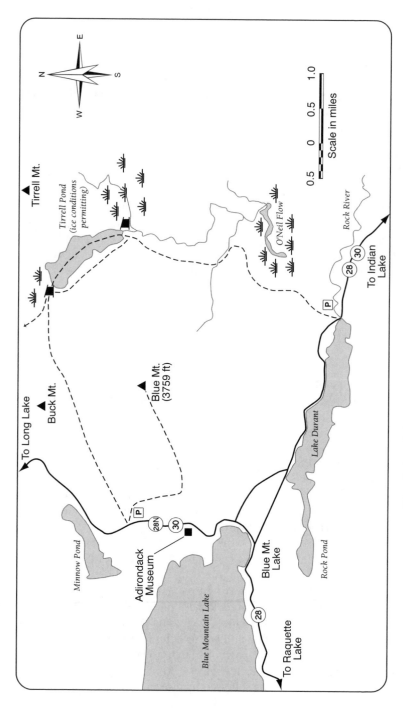

Tirrell Pond (Trip 27) and Blue Mountain (Trip 34)

return to state land at 3.4 mi.

O'Neil Flow Lean-to is reached at 3.5 mi at the south end of the pond. The lean-to at the north end of the pond is more likely to offer sun, and the surface of the pond offers great views of Blue Mountain and surrounding peaks. Thus, ice conditions permitting, cross the lake to the north end, a distance of approximately one mile.

One can also reach Tirrell Pond from the trailhead 0.1 mi north of the Adirondack Museum in Blue Mountain Lake. This route is approximately one mile longer, and the descent to Tirrell Pond from the height of land north of Blue Mountain requires a bit more than intermediate skill. However, starting at Blue Mountain Lake and skiing to the Northville-Placid Trail start is a nice 8.0 mi trip with a net descent of over four hundred vertical feet.

28. Stephens and Cascade Ponds

Distance: 6.6 mi (10.6 km) round-trip to Stephens Pond; 8.8 mi (14.2 km) loop trip to both ponds
Difficulty: Ski, intermediate; snowshoe, novice
Maps: Page 92. ADK Central Region; USGS Blue Mountain Lake
    metric series

There are many variations to these described trips depending on the inclination of the group and the condition of the ice on Lake Durant.

▶ If the ice conditions are safe and the surface suitable for skiing, one can make this a scenic and varied loop trip starting at Lake Durant Public Campground. If the trip over the ice is not feasible or one just wants to save 1.8 mi, then shuttle to Durant Road at the west end of the lake. Lake Durant Public Campground is on NY 28 and NY 30, 2.6 mi east of Blue Mountain Lake and approximately eight miles west of Indian Lake.

(The Durant Road start is found by driving 0.9 mi east from the intersection in Blue Mountain Lake and turning right onto Durant Road. Parking is at the trailhead on the left, 0.2 mi down Durant Road. Then go 0.1 mi down the narrow side road and turn right at the DEC sign to find the trail that leads to a slightly tricky descent to the bridge over Rock Pond.) ◀

From the Lake Durant parking lot (0.0 mi), ski west on the ice to the outlet of Rock Pond at 2.4 mi at the west end of the lake. Here one encounters the Cascade Pond Trail, which goes left, and with a bit of

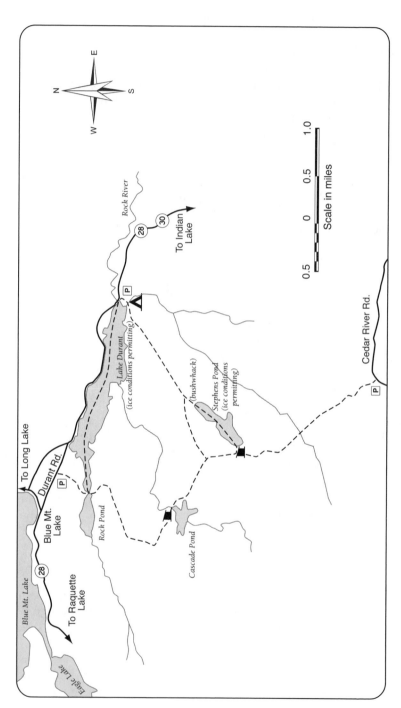

Stephens and Cascade Ponds (Trip 28)

steep going both up and down, gets over a ridge before turning west and up a beautiful valley. The trail steepens again at 3.6 mi, after which it levels out and swings east to the lean-to at the outlet of Cascade Pond at 4.6 mi. If ice conditions permit, the easiest route from the lean-to is to ski to the far end of the east bay of the pond. From there, it is an easy 100 yd bushwhack up to the trail. Otherwise, follow the markers across the outlet, after which the trail is at first level and then climbs to a junction with the Northville-Placid Trail (trail register) at 5.5 mi.

From here, one can turn left and return 2.7 mi to the starting point, but by turning right one descends to the lean-to on Stephens Pond at 6.1 mi. Again assuming ice conditions are favorable, one can return by skiing to the north end of Stephens Pond, from which a 0.3 mi bushwhack up a wide, gentle, and obvious valley leads to the Northville-Placid Trail at 7.0 mi. The trail now descends in gradual stages to Lake Durant at 8.8 mi.

The round-trip to Stephens Pond from Lake Durant Campground is an easy ski, but lacks the variety of scenery and terrain found on the full loop. The formerly popular alternative southern approach to Stephens Pond from McCanes on the Cedar River Rd. is no longer possible due to a change in ownership of the trailhead.

29. Snowy Mountain

Distance: 7.8 mi. (12.6 km) round-trip
Elevation change: 2106 ft (642 m)
Summit elevation: 3899 ft (1188 m)
Difficulty: Snowshoe, intermediate; ski, expert
Maps: Page 95. ADK Central Region; USGS Indian Lake metric series

At just 101 ft short of 4000 ft, Snowy Mountain is the highest peak in the southern half of the Adirondacks. Snowy is a popular winter trip, usually done as a snowshoe hike because the final 0.7 mi to the summit is steep enough to provide snowshoers with the same challenges found in the High Peaks. The woods are generally open up to the final steep pitch, however, which makes this a possible combined ski and snowshoe trip, adding interest and speed to the descent from the first view at 3.2 mi. Alternatively, because the grade increases at a generally steady rate, one can simply ski up to the "point of comfort" and then don snowshoes for the rest of the climb.

▶ The trailhead is on the west side of NY 30, 6.9 mi south of Indian Lake village and 4.5 mi north of Lewey Lake outlet. ◀

Marked with red DEC disks, the trail is fairly level to the first crossing of Beaver Brook at 1.2 mi. The trail steepens a bit, then eases before a second crossing of Beaver Brook at 1.9 mi. More brook crossings are encountered as the trail gradually steepens to the first lookout at 3.2 mi. From here it is very steep to the summit cliff at 3.9 mi. This cliff offers a wonderful view to the east, including Indian Lake.

Another 200 yd beyond the cliff is the actual summit, with a fire tower that has been restored and is again climbable. If winter conditions make climbing inadvisable, a side trail extends 50 yd west of the summit cliff view to provide a view to the west toward Squaw and Panther Mountains.

30. Hoffman Notch

Distance: 7.6 mi (12.3 km) round-trip to Big Marsh;
    7.4 mi (11.9 km) through trip to Blue Ridge Road (see cautions)
Elevation change: 540 ft (165 m)
High Point: 1740 ft (530 m)
Difficulty: Ski, novice to Big Marsh, intermediate beyond;
    snowshoe, novice to Big Marsh, intermediate beyond
Maps: Page 97. USGS Blue Ridge and Schroon Lake metric series

With steep ridges rising on both sides, Hoffman Notch offers some of the most spectacular winter scenery available in the Adirondacks. This route was once marked as a snowmobile trail, but this use ended after the area was designated as wilderness. Since then, maintenance has been spotty—especially north of Big Marsh—so those attempting a through trip may have difficulty with blowdown. In addition, the descent on the north side of the notch has three stream crossings without bridges, and the trail has not been brushed out to the full width of the original road, leaving less room to maneuver.

In 1995 DEC rerouted the first mile of the trail in from Blue Ridge Rd. at the north end of this trip. This reroute bypassed a difficult crossing of a beaver swamp. As of 2005, however, no further improvements have been made on the north side of the notch. The through trip thus requires two or more feet of snow and no recent thaws that might have complicated the brook crossings.

▶ The southern start is at the tiny cluster of houses known as Loch

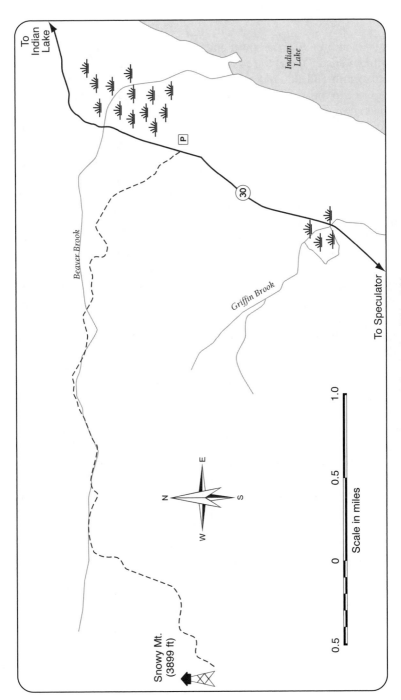

Snowy Mountain (Trip 29)

Muller. From US 9 at the south end of the village of Schroon Lake, take Hoffman Road 5.6 mi west to the junction of Potash Hill Rd. Turn right onto Potash Hill Rd. and again at the junction with Loch Muller Rd. Continue to the usual end of plowing at 2.2 mi from Hoffman Rd. If the plowing appears adequate beyond here, continue driving. Otherwise, park and ski 0.1 mi to a right turn leading in another 0.1 mi to the summer parking area. A DEC sign at the far end marks the start of both the Bailey Pond trail (left with blue markers) and the Hoffman Notch trail (right with yellow markers). ◄

From the DEC sign (0.0 mi) the trail begins by descending to the West Branch of Trout Brook (Bailey Pond outlet) at 0.4 mi. The trail crosses the brook on a bridge and then climbs across the south slope of Washburn Ridge. After crossing several small brooks, the trail descends to a junction on the west bank of the North Branch of Trout Brook at 1.2 mi. Here a trail leads right across a footbridge. This is an old snowmobile trail, now reopened as a footpath, leading to Big Pond—not to confused with this trip's destination of Big Marsh. (Many skiers coming from the north end have become confused here because this trail appears to be the route to Loch Muller as shown—incorrectly—on the 1953 USGS map.)

Bearing left at this junction (right, if coming from the north), the Hoffman Notch trail generally follows the bottom of a flat valley with much fresh beaver activity. At 3.8 mi the trail reaches the west shore of Big Marsh—in reality a sizable pond. From the surface of the pond there are excellent views of Texas Ridge, Hornet Cobbles, and Washburn Ridge.

For those continuing beyond Big Marsh, the going is flat for another 0.8 mi to Hoffman Notch Brook. From here one is faced with several potentially difficult brook crossings along with 500 ft of vertical descent before reaching an open field and power line at the base of the descent at 6.3 mi. The travel is again easy on the new route as one reaches a sturdy bridge over a large brook at 6.6 mi, followed by more bridges at 6.5 mi. After these bridges, the trail swings right and heads east as it climbs gently to Blue Ridge Road at 7.4 mi. This trailhead is on the south side of the road just west of a bridge over The Branch, 5.7 mi from Northway Exit 29 and 13.2 mi from NY 28N and the Tahawus Road.

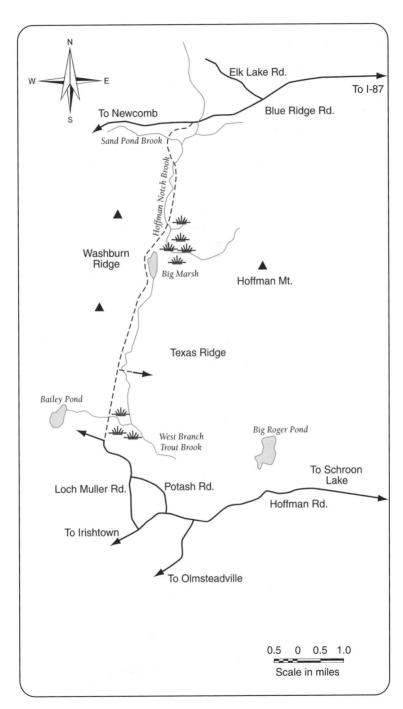

Hoffman Notch (Trip 30)

31. Cheney Pond and Lester Flow

Distance: 5.2 mi (8.4 km) round-trip
Difficulty: Ski, novice; snowshoe, beginner
Maps: ADK Central Region; USGS Blue Ridge metric series

Relatively easy terrain combined with some unusual views of the Great
Range make this a great little trip. It is, however, a long drive from just
about anywhere for a relatively short ski. On the plus side, as of 2004 the
snowmobile trail through to Irishtown was not being maintained, so
one can now usually ski to the view from Lester Dam without encountering snowmobiles. Whereas once one could return via the ice on Lester
Flow, the old dam at Lester Flow has now been breached and the current
in the Boreas River makes it far less likely that ice conditions will be
good enough to permit a return back up the open flow.

▶ The start is on Blue Ridge Road, 5.5 mi north and then east from
NY 28N and 13.5 mi west from Northway Exit 29. ◀

From Blue Ridge Road (0.0 mi), the road descends gradually to an
intersection at 0.4 mi. (The road left goes 0.3 mi to Cheney Pond.)
Bearing right, the route to Lester Flow dam soon reaches a barrier and

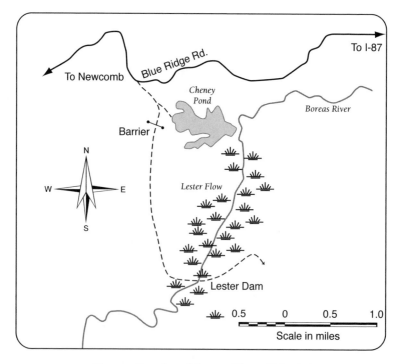

Cheney Pond and Lester Flow (Trip 31)

then an unmarked junction at 0.5 mi. Bear left and continue mostly on the level until a long, gradual descent leads to a large beaver dam on the right at 2.4 mi. Turning left at a junction at 2.5 mi, the route leads through a small campsite to the edge of Lester Flow at 2.6 mi. Looking to the north, one can see the Great Range with the bare rock faces of Basin and Gothics Mountains prominent.

When the large crib dam was in use, it created the large body of water shown on the older maps. Now there is only a small bit of slack water above the old dam and the former flow area is rapidly filling in with trees and shrubs. It is usually possible, however, to obtain an even better view by crossing the Boreas River to the rocky bluffs on the east side. Pick the crossing carefully; there is considerable current in the river that can cause thin ice. If one does attempt the trip back up the open flow and across Cheney Pond, most if not all the skiing should be in the thick alders and occasional meadows beside the river until one reaches Cheney Pond.

32. Stony Pond

Distance: 4.2 mi (6.8 km) round-trip; 6.0 mi (9.7 km) point-to-point
Difficulty: Ski, intermediate; snowshoe, novice
Maps: Page 100. ADK Central Region; USGS Newcomb and Blue Ridge metric series

The trips as described below are but two of several excellent possibilities in this area. There are several smaller ponds to explore, and Green Mountain can make a good destination for a combined ski and snowshoe trip. The through trip offers skiers over 900 ft of net vertical descent, although a few short pitches are on the high side of intermediate for skiers.

This area has also seen some snowmobile traffic in recent years, although from the comments by snowmobilers in the lean-to register it doesn't appear any of them will be coming back. This road-width trail is fine for skiers, but is apparently too narrow for the liking of some snowmobilers. Furthermore, the start of the trail off NY 28N is apparently difficult because one must get a machine up over the snow banks as well as climb the first hill.

▶ The start is on NY 28N, 3.9 mi north of its junction with the Olmsteadville Road. (To find the Irishtown end of the through trip, turn left, if coming from the north, off NY 28N on the Minerva-

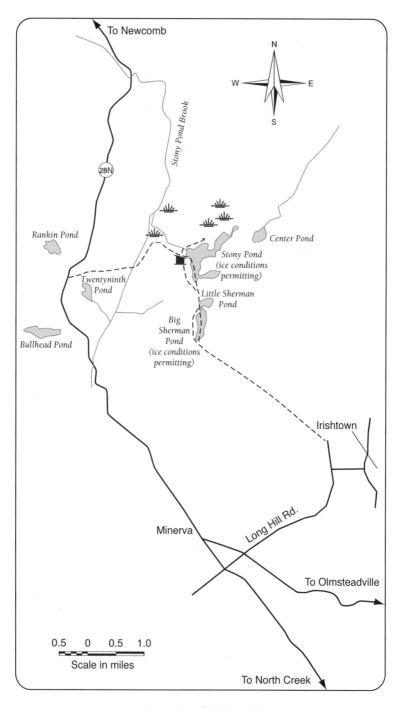

Stony Pond (Trip 32)

Olmsteadville Road and then left on Long Hill Road south of the center of Minerva. It is 1.7 mi to a junction, which one passes straight through to the east trailhead at 2.1 mi from the Minerva-Olmsteadville Road.)◀

From NY 28N (0.0 mi), the trail starts up a short grade, but soon levels off. A vague trail goes right at 0.3 mi (to a campsite and Twentyninth Pond) as the main trail descends gently through a spruce swamp. Just beyond, the trail climbs moderately to a height of land at 0.5 mi. This is the steepest climb/descent on the trail to Stony Pond, and fortunately the trail is also its widest on this pitch. After the height of land, there is a longer descent, first to one brook crossing at 0.8 mi and then to the bottom of the valley and where the trail crosses Stony Pond Brook at 1.0 mi. From here the trail climbs in stages past several beaver ponds to the lean-to on Stony Pond at 2.1 mi.

To continue through to Irishtown, proceed to the south end of the pond. The trail is found to the right at the only break in the trees on this thickly wooded shoreline. The trail then climbs slightly before descending a short, steep, and somewhat difficult pitch to Little Sherman Pond at 2.8 mi. One can now continue to the south end of Big Sherman Pond and find the trail on the east shore near the outlet at 3.0 mi. Turning right at the junction with the trail that runs along the east shore, the descent to Irishtown soon begins. At 3.6 mi yellow paint blazes indicate a small inholding of private land and a private trail going right. After a short, steep pitch at 4.3 mi the steady grade resumes to the end of the trail at 6.0 mi.

33. Goodnow Mountain

Distance: 3.8 mi (6.1 km) round-trip
Elevation change: 1060 ft (323 m)
Summit elevation: 2690 ft (820 m)
Difficulty: Snowshoe, novice; ski, intermediate-expert
Map: Page 102. USGS Newcomb metric series

Goodnow Mountain is a little gem in any season as it combines a short hike on a well-maintained trail with a spectacular view. This trip is entirely on the property of the Archer and Anna Huntington Wildlife Forest Station, which is part of the SUNY College of Environmental Science and Forestry in Syracuse. The Station has restored the fire tower on the summit so that one's view can be further enhanced with a climb to the top—assuming the steps are not prohibitively icy. In 1993 the trail

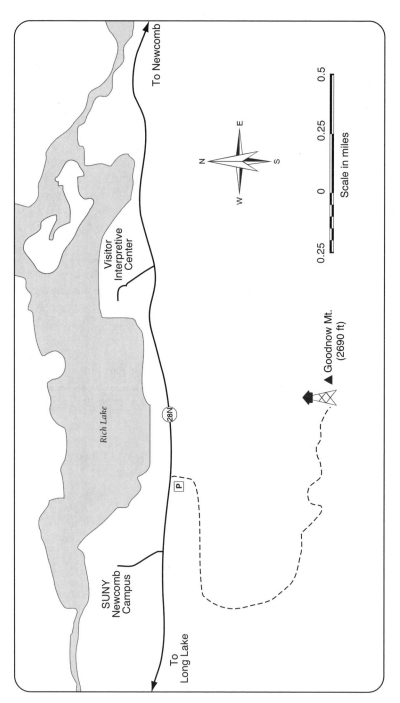

Goodnow Mountain (Trip 33)

was rerouted onto its present line. This reroute created a superior hiking trail, but the narrow width of some pitches in the midsection of the route make this a better snowshoe hike than ski tour.

▶ The trail starts on the south side of NY 28N 1.5 mi west of the entrance to the Visitor Interpretive Center west of Newcomb. This point is also 11.6 mi east of Long Lake village. A large white sign marks the parking lot. ◀

The trail, which follows red markers, climbs moderately for about two hundred yards before swinging right and along a shelf parallel to the highway. There is a bridge over a small brook at 0.5 mi, after which the trail swings left and up. Moderate climbing begins at 0.7 mi and continues to the crest of a ridge at 0.9 mi, where the new trail joins the old trail. Now on an old woods road, the trail climbs at a steady, gradual grade until it levels off in a notch at 1.5 mi. There is a small horse barn on the right. From here, the trail climbs gradually to the crest of the ridge, dips down, and then climbs gradually to the tower on the summit at 1.9 mi.

There are some views to the east and south without climbing the tower, but from the tower one can see twenty-three of the major peaks, with the Santanoni Range, Algonquin Peak, and Mt. Marcy particularly prominent.

34. Blue Mountain

Distance: 4.0 mi (6.5 km) round-trip
Elevation change: 1550 ft (473 m)
Summit elevation: 3759 ft (1146 m)
Difficulty: Snowshoe, intermediate; ski, expert
Maps: Page 90. ADK Central Region; USGS Blue Mountain Lake
    metric series

As noted in *Guide to Adirondack Trails: Central Region*, Blue Mountain has been one of the most frequently climbed Adirondack peaks for over a century. In recent years this has extended throughout the winter season as well as summer. As a result, the trail often is broken out shortly after a storm, but if it isn't, one is likely have help coming along from behind to share the trail-breaking duties.

The fire tower on the summit has been restored and the views from the top of the tower are superb, although there are good views without climbing the tower. The summit is on private land, which means that there are a number of additional communications towers on the summit that detract somewhat from the experience. The views, however, encompass such a tremendous sweep of wilderness lakes and mountains that one can easily ignore the civilized clutter in the foreground. The service road (actually a steep tractor track) for all these communications towers on the north side of the mountain is posted as private.

▶ The start is on NY 30 and NY 28N 1.4 mi north of the NY 30/28/28N intersection in Blue Mountain Lake village. This is also 0.1 mi up the hill from the entrance to the Adirondack Museum. As an interesting bit of trivia, at 2200 ft elevation this is the highest point on any continuous highway in New York State. This is also the start for the alternate approach to Tirrell Pond (see Trip 27, page 90). ◀

The Blue Mountain trail, marked with red DEC disks, goes right and heads east on the flat from the trailhead. At first following an old logging road, the trail gains elevation gradually before turning right and crossing a brook at 0.3 mi. Continuing to gain elevation as it traverses across the side of the mountain, the trail steepens at 0.9 mi to gain the crest of a ridge. This is the ridge followed by the original trail that started closer to the village.

The grade on the ridge is at first gradual, but soon steepens with several views to the west possible through bare trees. Under some conditions of major thaw and freeze, crampons may be desirable on this steepest part of the climb. At 1.5 mi, the grade eases as the trail winds through a spruce forest to the summit at 2.0 mi.

West-Central Region

Perhaps the most significant feature of the West-Central region is that Old Forge usually leads the Adirondacks in total annual snowfall. The region also has miles and miles of trails leading to dozens of picturesque ponds and small rocky summits. The area's drawback is such an abundance of snowmobilers that skiers and snowshoers may sometimes feel like unwelcome visitors. Within this mecca for motorized recreation, however, lie two of the Adirondacks's larger wilderness areas, Ha-de-ron-dah and Pigeon Lake, as well as numerous other trails on which motorized vehicles are prohibited.

None of the West-Central region trips in this guide use snowmobile trails because recent improvements (some quite controversial) to just about every available designated snowmobile trail have made these routes unattractive for nonmotorized users. One example of these changes is the Safford Pond trail. Ten years ago it was a narrow route used by only a few snowmobiles each year; today it is twenty to thirty feet wide and a major thoroughfare between Old Forge and Big Moose. Skiers also should be aware that skiing is prohibited on snowmobile trails on private land.

There are currently three developed areas for cross-country skiing in the Old Forge–Inlet area. Adirondack Woodcraft is based at a summer camp located west of Old Forge. McCauley Mountain, a downhill ski center, has several loops of up to approximately three miles (five kilometers) at the base of the mountain that are the site for several races during the course of each winter. Fern Park, operated by the Town of Inlet, offers the most extensive network of groomed trails, including one and one-fifth mile (two kilometers) of lighted trails for night skiing.

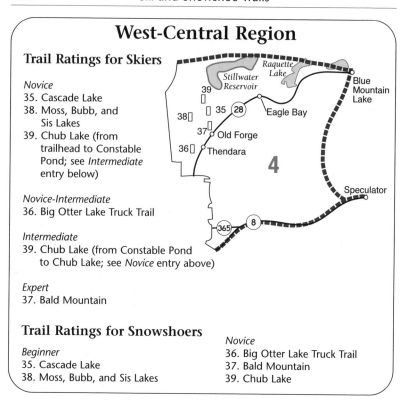

West-Central Region

Trail Ratings for Skiers

Novice
35. Cascade Lake
38. Moss, Bubb, and
    Sis Lakes
39. Chub Lake (from
    trailhead to Constable
    Pond; see *Intermediate*
    entry below)

Novice-Intermediate
36. Big Otter Lake Truck Trail

Intermediate
39. Chub Lake (from Constable Pond
    to Chub Lake; see *Novice* entry above)

Expert
37. Bald Mountain

Trail Ratings for Snowshoers

Beginner
35. Cascade Lake
38. Moss, Bubb, and Sis Lakes

Novice
36. Big Otter Lake Truck Trail
37. Bald Mountain
39. Chub Lake

West-Central Region Cross-Country Ski Centers and Sites
Adirondack Woodcraft Ski Touring Center 315-369-6031
Fern Park Recreation Area 315-357-5501
McCauley Mountain 315-369-3225

35. Cascade Lake

Distance: 2.4 mi (3.8 km) round-trip; 6.0 mi (9.7 km) loop
Difficulty: Ski, novice; snowshoe, beginner
Maps: ADK West-Central Region; USGS Eagle Bay metric series

Offering easy going on a mostly road-width trail, a beautiful lake for a destination, and a variety of possible distances including a waterfall, this trip is an ideal introduction to the region.

▶ The new start, which has better and safer parking, is located beyond the original start on Big Moose Road. The current parking is 1.3

mi west of NY 28 in Eagle Bay on the right. ◀

From the trailhead (0.0 mi), a new piece of trail goes east and parallel to Big Moose Road heading back towards Eagle Bay for about 0.2 mi to the trail register. The new trail goes up over a hill and down a moderate to steep grade and is by far the most difficult terrain on the trip. The trail is marked with yellow DEC ski trail disks and an occasional red marker.

From the register, gentle grades on an old road lead first up and then down to a junction at 1.0 mi, just before a large meadow. If one's goal is just the 2.4 mi tour to the lake and back, turn left at this junction and glide down to the outlet of Cascade Lake at 1.2 mi. To make the complete circuit of the lake, bear right at this junction. At first the trail is mostly level across a slope before gently descending to a brook at 3.0 mi.

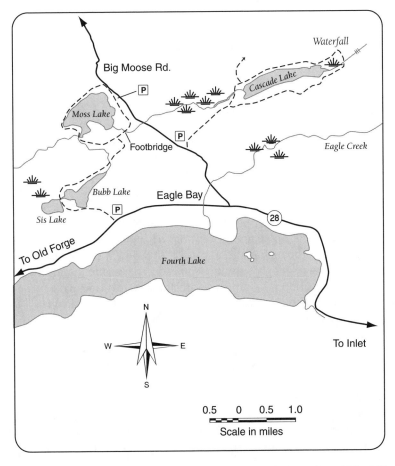

Cascade Lake (Trip 35) and Moss, Bubb, and Sis Lakes (Trip 38)

(A short bushwhack up this brook brings one to a high, narrow waterfall from which the lake derives its name.) With less than perfect snow cover, it may be difficult to cross this major inlet to Cascade Lake or to cross several smaller streams just beyond. If the crossings are too difficult, one can always turn around; but under good conditions the continuation makes an enjoyable loop.

About one mile after crossing the major brook, one comes to some overgrown fields that were once part of a summer camp. These fields are followed at 4.2 mi by a beautiful open point with a designated campsite. At 4.7 mi a red-marked trail diverges right, but bear left and down to a crossing of the outlet to Cascade Lake at 4.8 mi. One then climbs gently up to the right of the open field to the junction with the trail one started on at 5.0 mi. Turn right to return to the road at 6.0 mi.

36. Big Otter Lake Truck Trail

Distance: Up to 17.4 mi (28.1 km) round-trip
Difficulty: Ski, novice-intermediate; snowshoe, novice
Maps: ADK West-Central Region; USGS Thendara metric series

A few years ago, one of the major ski manufacturers adopted the slogan "as far as you want to go." They must have had this area in mind; the gently rolling terrain traversed by this truck trail invites one to push on and on. Those who manage to ski all the way to Big Otter Lake will have crossed the Ha-de-ron-dah Wilderness Area and returned. Because crossing the wilderness leads one to more snowmobile trails at the west end, however, there is no shame in settling for a round-trip ski to Indian Brook (3.0 mi), the high point on the side of Moose River Mountain (6.0 mi), or the newly reopened summit of Moose River Mountain (5.6 mi) at 2018 ft elevation. The obvious attractions of this tour have made it quite popular with skiers, and one may expect to have broken track for at least part of the way—usually to the high point on Moose River Mountain.

▶ The start is in Thendara, on a side road leading north from NY 28 just west of the railroad underpass. Follow this road 0.4 mi to its end, where there is a parking area. ◀

From the parking area (0.0 mi), the route runs concurrently with a heavily used snowmobile trail for a few yards before turning left and up to a barrier gate and register at 0.3 mi. (Use caution descending this hill on the return; snowmobile traffic can be heavy.) Past the barrier gate, a

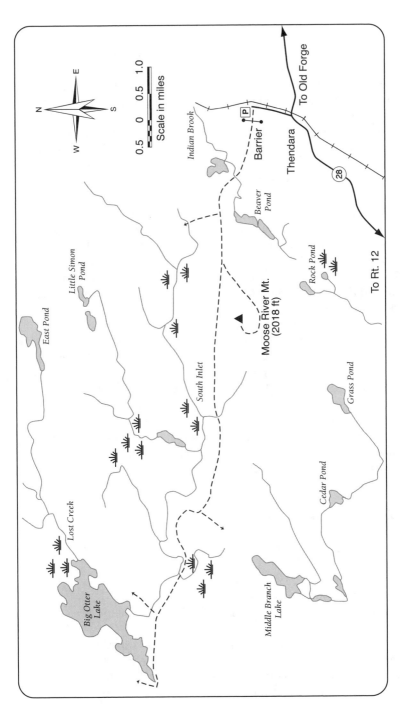

Big Otter Lake Truck Trail (Trip 36)

series of ups and downs lead to a longer descent to an open wetland at 1.0 mi. This is followed first by a crossing of Indian Brook and then by the junction with the East Pond–Lost Creek Trail at 1.5 mi. Bearing left, the truck trail begins a gradual climb up a ridge. At 2.2 mi the truck trail reaches a junction.

(The trail going straight ahead is the newly reopened road to the summit of Moose River Mountain. This trail climbs gradually for 0.6 mi to the summit, which in winter offers some views through the trees, making this an attractive destination. Skiers will particularly enjoy the more than mile-long coast back to the East Pond Trail.)

The truck trail swings right at this junction and continues a gentle climb across the slope with occasional views to the north. At 3.0 mi the truck trail begins to descend and then flattens before reaching a junction with a trail left to Middle Branch and Middle Settlement Lakes at 4.9 mi. Bearing right, a short climb and descent lead to a large open area at 5.9 mi and the junction with the Lost Creek trail at 6.5 mi. Continuing on, the truck trail ends at 7.4 mi.

For skiers, the best route by which to continue from the end of the truck trail is an unmarked wood road going right just before the end of the truck trail and leading to Big Otter Lake at 7.5 mi. The Big Otter Lake East Trail continues as a footpath before reaching the west boundary of the wilderness area at 7.8 mi. (It is possible to continue via the Big Otter West Trail to a trailhead 3.7 mi beyond Big Otter Lake to make a point-to-point tour of 11.2 mi; but, given that more time would likely be spent in a very long shuttle, and that the west end is a frequently used snowmobile trail, this is not as attractive an option as the long, easy ski back in one's tracks.)

37. Bald Mountain

Distances: 2.0 mi (3.2 km) round-trip
Elevation change: 390 ft (119 m)
Summit elevation: 2350 ft (716 m)
Difficulty: Snowshoe, novice; ski, expert
Maps: ADK West-Central Region; USGS Old Forge metric series

Bald Mountain is high on just about every list of trips offering "greatest reward for least effort." The trail has a few steeper spots that will challenge beginning snowshoers, and after a major thaw-freeze cycle crampons may be needed on the areas of open rock. Nevertheless, the short

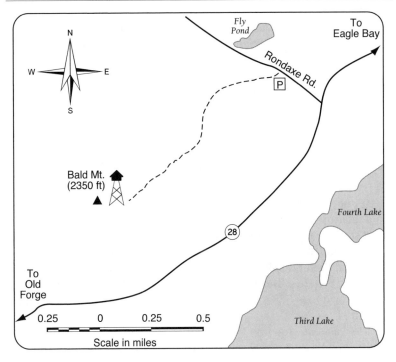

Bald Mountain (Trip 37)

distance makes this trip available to every level of snowshoer. There are good views from the rocky summit, and the tower is in good enough shape to climb for a truly superior view. On particularly clear days, Mt. Marcy and other of the higher peaks are visible from the summit and with their white domes are much easier to pick out in winter than in summer.

▶ The start is on Rondaxe Road, which leaves NY 28 4.5 mi north of the Tourist Information Center in Old Forge or 4.5 mi south of the village of Eagle Bay. The parking area is 0.2 mi from NY 28 on the left. ◀

From the parking area (0.0 mi) the trail begins at a moderate grade through a deciduous forest, but the grade soon steepens as the trail climbs up through an attractive spruce-fir forest. The first views of parts of the Fulton Chain of lakes begin at 0.4 mi. The final part of the ascent is a mostly moderate grade along the rocky spine of the ridge to the base of the fire tower at 0.9 mi. The trail continues for another 0.1 mi to an additional vantage point. Beyond this vantage point is private land and an almost never-used snowmobile trail descends to connect with one of

the main routes in the Old Forge snowmobile trail system. (As noted in
the introduction to this region, skiing is prohibited on these trails.)

38. Moss, Bubb, and Sis Lakes

Distance: 2.5 mi (4.0 km) round-trip to Moss Lake; 5.3 mi (8.5 km)
    round-trip to Moss, Bubb, and Sis Lakes
Difficulty: Ski, novice; snowshoe, beginner
Maps: Page 107. ADK West-Central Region; USGS Eagle Bay metric series

As described, this trip circles Moss Lake on the Circuit Trail with a possible side trip to Bubb and Sis Lakes. As a round-trip, it has the simplic-
ity of starting and finishing at the same point. One can also do this as a
4.0 mi point-to-point trip starting on NY 28, going past Sis and Bubb
Lakes, and then finishing with the circuit around Moss Lake. For skiers,
this is the preferred direction for the point-to-point trip because the 0.2
mi hill down to NY 28 is quite rough and not particularly suited for a ski
descent.

Moss Lake was for fifty years the site of a girl's camp before being
acquired by the State of New York in 1973. Shortly afterwards, the area
was occupied by Mohawk settlers pursuing land claims against the State.
There was a lengthy confrontation that was much in the news at the
time. The standoff finally ended when then Secretary of State Mario
Cuomo negotiated an agreement by which the Mohawks moved to the
Macomb State Reservation—a piece of state land outside the Adirondack
Park near Plattsburgh. An interpretive display at the trailhead provides
additional details on the history of this area.

▶ The trailhead is on Big Moose Road, 2.1 mi from NY 28 in Eagle
Bay. There is a (usually) plowed parking area on the left. ◀

From the parking area, follow yellow markers to the left, passing several roads, once part of the camp complex, that lead toward the lake. At
0.3 mi the trail crosses a field with weather instruments, followed by
another road to the left at 0.4 mi. (This leads to the old winter parking
area on Big Moose Road that was used before the present parking area
was regularly plowed.) Bearing right, the Circuit Trail descends to cross
Moss Lake's main inlet on a bridge, followed by two short climbs and
descents to the junction with the Bubb Lake Trail on the left at 0.7 mi.

(Bubb Lake is an easy side trip mostly on the flat. At 0.5 mi from the
Moss Lake Trail, one crosses Bubb Lake's outlet with a fish barrier dam
just below the bridge. Reaching Bubb Lake in another 0.2 mi one can

simply enjoy the view of Onondaga Mountain from the hemlock stand or, ice conditions permitting, ski another 0.7 mi to the south end and over to Sis Lake.)

From the junction with the Bubb Lake Trail, the Circuit Trail continues to a crossing of Moss Lake's outlet at 1.2 mi. This offers the only good view of the lake from the Circuit Trail. After rounding the southwest corner of the lake, the trail climbs gradually up across a steep side hill. At 2.0 mi, the first of several old roads lead toward the lake, and at 2.3 mi the trail makes a sharp right turn to parallel Big Moose Road back to the starting point at 2.5 mi.

39. Chub Lake

Distance: 6.0 mi (9.7 km) round-trip
Difficulty: Ski, novice to Constable Pond, intermediate to Chub Lake; snowshoe, novice
Maps: Page 114. ADK West-Central Region; USGS Eagle Bay metric series

Chub Lake is but one of many attractive ponds in the Pigeon Lake Wilderness Area that one can visit without having to share the trail with snowmobiles. This trip follows the most skiable of the whole network of trails linking Pigeon, Queer, and Cascade Lakes, and Mays, Chain, and Windfall Ponds. (Each of these other trails either has a few steep spots or suffers from lack of maintenance, but all can and have been skied and all make excellent snowshoe trips.) This trip does not see as much winter use as neighboring Cascade Lake or Moss Lake, so trail breaking may be a consideration.

▶ Starting from NY 28 in Eagle Bay, drive 3.8 mi on Big Moose Road and then turn right on Higby Road for 1.3 mi to Judson Road, a private, unplowed road. Park on Higby Road just before or after the junction at whatever spot appears to be the widest. There is no trailhead sign and there are no markers for the first 0.2 mi. ◀

From Higby Road (0.0 mi) the route follows Judson Road for 0.2 mi and then bears right (blue markers) just before Judson Road turns left to cross Constable Creek. A few yards after this right turn, one comes to a vehicle barrier and register. The trail then follows an old road along the bank of Constable Creek to a junction at 0.5 mi with a side trail going right to Queer Lake. Continuing straight ahead 75 yd beyond this junction, the route crosses Constable Creek and narrows until it meets a road at 0.9 mi. (One short, steep pitch on this narrow section is, for skiers, the

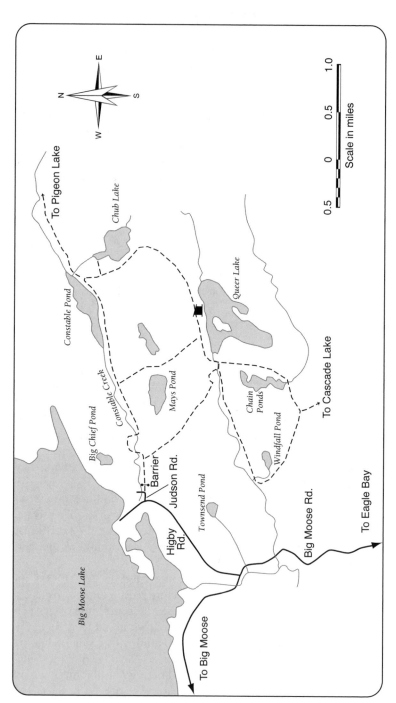

Chub Lake (Trip 39)

only non-novice hill on the trip as far as Constable Pond.) Turning right on this road, the route soon recrosses Constable Creek on a lumber bridge. Turning left after this bridge, the blue-marked route leaves the road and soon reaches state land.

At 1.3 mi a side trail to Mays Pond goes right. Continuing straight ahead at this junction, there is a nice stretch of trail next to the open wetland along Constable Creek, or one can choose to make a short bushwhack down to the creek and proceed along its open banks. If one stays on the trail, Constable Pond is first visible on the left at 2.2 mi, and a short spur trail diverges left to Constable Pond at 2.5 mi.

Fifty yards beyond this spur trail, the blue-marked trail comes to a junction with a yellow-marked trail leading right to Chub Lake. (The trail straight ahead leads to Pigeon Lake, but recent lack of maintenance makes it a less-than-perfect winter route.) Turning right at the junction, one climbs slightly, descends, and climbs again to a junction at 2.8 mi. To reach Chub Lake, one can either turn left at this junction and follow the trail for 0.2 mi to the northwest shore of the lake, or one can bear right and continue down for 0.2 mi to a crossing of an inlet to Chub Lake (with the lake clearly visible to the left). With either option one reaches the lake at 3.0 mi.

Southern Region

Although the southern Adirondacks is accessible to large numbers of potential skiers and snowshoers, there has not been as much winter activity in the region as a whole as one might expect. The area from Benson to Speculator often has good snow, but only a few of the trips described here regularly see much winter use—at least nonmotorized use.

The limitation may be that the area's centerpiece, the Silver Lake Wilderness Area, has only the Northville-Placid Trail as a major trail. The adjoining Wilcox Lake, Ferris Lake, and Shaker Mountain Wild Forest Areas have more trails, but most of them are designated snowmobile trails. Not all of these snowmobile trails are heavily trafficked, however, and for skiers there are some appealing destinations to be discovered beyond the frequently used Rock Lake tour.

The Wilcox Lake trail receives heavy snowmobile use and thus is not included here, but it appears for now that the other snowmobile trails on Forest Preserve land in this region will remain primitive—i.e., narrow and rarely used by snowmobiles. For snowshoers, the snowshoe hike up Hadley Mountain is an excellent trip and a highlight of this region.

Lapland Lake in Benson is the only cross-country ski center in the region, but it is one of the Adirondacks's most established centers, with a well-deserved reputation for consistently having the best snow conditions in the Adirondacks. Piseco and Speculator also maintain small ski loops (permit required), although snowmobiling is the primary winter recreation in these two towns.

Southern Region Cross-Country Ski Center and Sites
Lapland Lake 518-863-4974
Speculator/Piseco area 518-548-4521

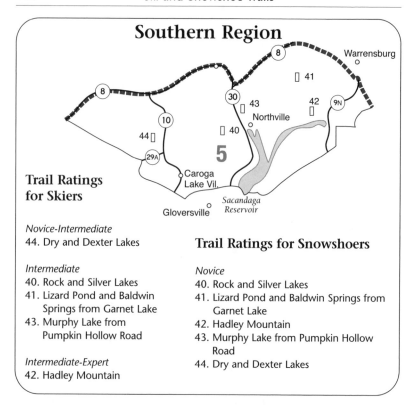

Southern Region

Trail Ratings for Skiers

Novice-Intermediate
44. Dry and Dexter Lakes

Intermediate
40. Rock and Silver Lakes
41. Lizard Pond and Baldwin Springs from Garnet Lake
43. Murphy Lake from Pumpkin Hollow Road

Intermediate-Expert
42. Hadley Mountain

Trail Ratings for Snowshoers

Novice
40. Rock and Silver Lakes
41. Lizard Pond and Baldwin Springs from Garnet Lake
42. Hadley Mountain
43. Murphy Lake from Pumpkin Hollow Road
44. Dry and Dexter Lakes

40. Rock and Silver Lakes

Distance: 9.2 mi (14.8 km) round-trip to Rock Lake; 15.0 mi (24.2 km) round-trip to Silver Lake
Elevation change: 840 ft (255 m)
High-point elevation: 2140 ft (650 m)
Difficulty: Ski, intermediate; snowshoe, novice
Maps: Page 120. ADK Southern Region; USGS Three Ponds Mountain metric series

This is the most popular trip in the region, offering wilderness trails, several attractive destinations, and a nice downhill run for skiers on the return. Its proximity to Lapland Lake Cross-Country Ski Center provides an option for less ambitious skiers or snowshoers in a group, or an alternative in the event that groomed snow is preferable to the prevailing backcountry conditions. The route is the first part of the 132 mi Northville-Placid Trail. If skiing, one should be able to return in about two-thirds of the time required to reach any of these destinations, but do make note of any troublesome brook crossings so as to avoid unpleasant surprises on the return trip.

▶ The access is from NY 30 between Northville and Wells. Turn onto Benson Road, marked with signs for both the Northville-Placid Trail and Lapland Lake Cross-Country Ski Center. At 5.2 mi a road goes right to Lapland Lake, but bear left. At 5.8 mi the road crosses an iron bridge over West Stony Creek. Bear right immediately after the bridge, and then at 6.6 mi bear left onto Godfrey Road. The official parking lot is on the right, just over 7.0 mi from NY 30 with the register on the left, just beyond, at the junction with a private driveway. However, the road is now plowed another 200 yd to a new house with parking also possible here ($1.00 donation requested). ◀

From the official parking lot (0.0 mi), blue DEC markers lead gently down to a trail register on the left. Here the trail goes right on a plowed driveway past a new house and then down to a hunting camp belonging to the United Rod and Gun Club. This is clearly posted as private property and one must remain on the trail, for which there is a public easement.

The trail is flat for 0.2 mi and then makes a short, moderate-to-steep climb that is a good test of one's wax and technique because this ascent is as steep as any hill as far as Rock Lake. Partway up this hill, the road splits, then rejoins at the top, after which gentle grades lead up and then down to the bank of West Stony Creek at 1.2 mi. Turning sharp left in the clearing that was once a parking area, the trail passes an old cable barrier and arrives at a bridge over the North Branch of West Stony Creek at 1.5 mi.

The trail now climbs steadily to a crossing of Goldmine Creek at 2.4 mi. This section of trail is somewhat rocky and eroded and may be rough with marginal snow cover, but after Goldmine Creek the trail improves as it descends a bit before climbing again to a height of land at 3.2 mi. The trail then descends easily, climbs again, and reaches the junction with the side trail to Rock Lake at 4.5 mi. There is no sign for the side trail that leads 0.1 mi left to a small clearing, once the site of a lean-to. (Should one miss this junction, Rock Lake is soon visible through the trees on the left.)

[This trip to Rock Lake can be extended by about 1.5 mi by skiing to the west end of Rock Lake and then continuing 0.5 mi through the marshy area next to the outlet. Then turn right (north) and ski up to the head of a second marshy area. A short bushwhack leads to the Northville-Placid Trail. Turning right on the N-P Trail, a ski of just under

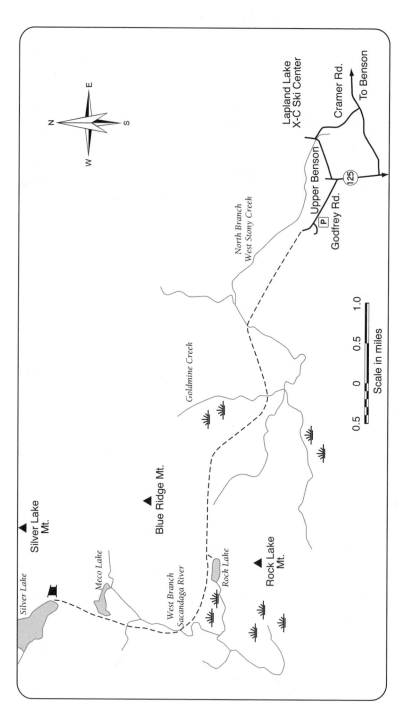

Rock and Silver Lakes (Trip 40)

one mile brings one back to the junction with the Rock Lake side trail.] The more ambitious can continue on to Meco Lake or the lean-to at Silver Lake. The trail between Rock Lake and the crossing of the West Branch of the Sacandaga River offers a few yards of difficult going, but otherwise the travel is straightforward and quite a few have ventured beyond Rock Lake in recent years. Beyond Rock Lake, the trail climbs around the west end of a hill after which there are a few short descents through balsam thickets before reaching an old lumber clearing at 5.5 mi. Just beyond this clearing, the trail crosses the West Branch of the Sacandaga River, turns sharp right, and begins to climb along an old road near the river.

There are numerous lovely waterfalls to be seen in this section before the trail pulls away from the river at 5.8 mi and continues climbing to the south shore of Meco Lake at 6.7 mi. The hiking trail follows the rough west shore and then climbs over a steep ridge at the north end, but, ice conditions permitting, one can cross the lake and follow the north inlet up past several beaver ponds for about three hundred yards to regain the trail where it crosses the inlet. From here, the trail is flat for another 300 yd before descending to the southeast bay of Silver Lake. The lean-to is just across this bay at 7.5 mi.

41. Lizard Pond and Baldwin Springs from Garnet Lake

Distance: 4.0 mi (6.5 km) round-trip to Lizard Lake lean-to; 10.3 mi (16.6 km) round-trip to Baldwin Springs
Difficulty: Ski, intermediate; snowshoe, novice
Maps: Page 122. ADK Southern Region; USGS Bakers Mills metric series

Although most of this tour is relatively flat, for skiers the initial 0.5 mi climb from Garnet Lake to Lizard Pond (misspelled Lixard on many maps) requires solid intermediate-level skills to negotiate. This section of trail is also a bit rough and requires a foot or more of solid base before being skiable.

Lizard Pond is a particularly attractive destination, and continuing on to Baldwin Springs offers a very pleasant trip through a variety of forest types. Baldwin Springs itself is on a popular snowmobile route between Harrisburg and NY 8, but this particular route via Lizard Pond, although designated as a snowmobile trail, is not often used by vehicles.

▶ The start is a small DEC boat-launching site on Garnet Lake. From

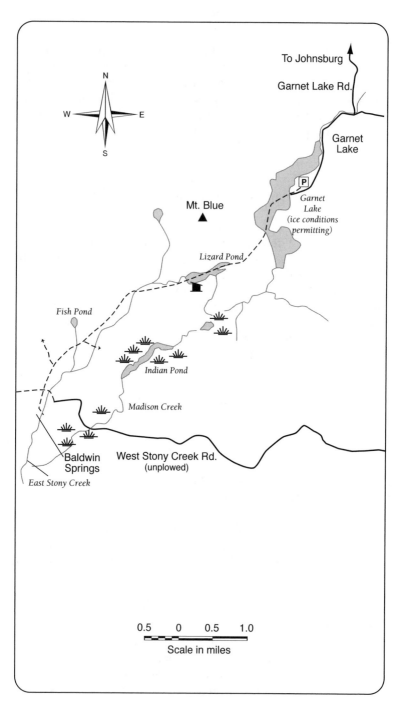

Lizard Pond and Baldwin Springs (Trip 41)

NY 8 in Johnsburg, take Garnet Lake Road approximately 6.0 mi south-west to a right turn up to the dam at the end of Garnet Lake. From the dam it is 0.9 mi on a narrow but usually passable road to the parking area at the boat-launching site. ◀

From the parking area (0.0 mi), head southwest on the lake for 0.7 mi to the narrowest part of the lake. The trail to Lizard Pond starts on the west shore of Garnet Lake, directly across from the point of the peninsula on the east shore. The trail is marked with snowmobile trail markers.

From the lake, the trail climbs moderately with a few breaks to the east end of the Lizard Pond marsh at 1.3 mi from the parking area. The trail skirts the south side of the marsh, but the easiest winter travel is across the marsh and west across the lake to the lean-to near the west end at 2.0 mi. From here one can see both the nearby rocky slopes of Mt. Blue and the more distant prominence of Crane Mountain.

Beyond the end of Lizard Pond the trail is less defined, but the wet areas encountered by summer hikers present little problem in the winter. From the west end of the pond, the trail descends slightly, traverses a small ridge, and then crosses two bridges at 2.6 mi. The trail now turns left and follows down the right bank of the outlet to Lizard Pond. After crossing several more streams, the trail enters a thick stand of tall hemlocks at 3.2 mi followed by tall pines at 3.5 mi. At 4.4 mi, signs mark the junction with a snowmobile trail leading left to Indian Pond. (This trail is not shown on the ADK hiking map as it is overgrown and cross-es too much wet ground to be passable in summer.) Turning right, the trail to Baldwin Springs soon crosses another stream on a good bridge and then passes two enormous glacial erratics on the right.

Beyond these erratics, the character of the land changes as one enters an area of sandy pine barrens. At 4.9 mi the Lizard Pond Trail reaches a junction with the Bartman Trail coming in from the north past Fish Pond. Turn left and continue for another 0.2 mi to a bridge over Stony Creek, with the main clearing at Baldwin Springs just beyond at 5.1 mi. Here there is a register and the junction with the well-used Cod Pond snowmobile trail. There was once a short-lived, tiny settlement here in lumbering days, but little evidence of it now remains.

Woods Lake, Lapland Lake Cross-Country Ski Center

42. Hadley Mountain

Distance: 3.6 mi (5.8 km) round-trip
Elevation change: 1525 ft (465 m)
Summit elevation: 2675 ft (815 m)
Difficulty: Snowshoe, novice; ski, intermediate-expert
Maps: ADK Southern Region; USGS Conklingville and
    Stony Creek 7.5' sheets

This is a delightful trip to a bald summit with a great view and a restored fire tower that provides even more outstanding views. The trail is road-width most of the way to the top, so although the trip is recommended for snowshoes, it is possible to ski it with two or more feet of snow and soft surface conditions. In really icy conditions, crampons may be required for snowshoers, but the trail is never steep enough to be technically difficult even after a severe thaw-freeze cycle. An interpretive brochure to this trail is usually available in the register box, although not all features described are visible in winter.

▶ To reach the start, take NY 9N to the center of Lake Luzerne. Turn west and cross the Hudson River to Hadley and then turn north on Stony Creek Road (Saratoga County Route 1) for 3.0 mi to Hadley Hill Road. Turn left (west) and proceed up Hadley Hill Road for 4.6 mi and turn right onto Tower Road for another 1.5 mi to the trailhead on the left. ◀

Marked with red DEC disks, the trail immediately begins a moderate climb. The grade eases briefly at a stream crossing at 0.5 mi but soon resumes its steady climb past cliffs on the right that often have colorful, blue-green ice formations. The trail then steepens for the final few hundred yards to the top of the ridge at 1.0 mi. Swinging right at the top of the ridge, the trail is flat for a bit before resuming a moderate climb culminating in a climb between cliffs to a clearing in a col at 1.3 mi. Here the marked trail swings left, bypassing the remnants straight ahead of a former route that followed the old telephone line. The relatively new route to the left offers spectacular views from ledges. The trail reaches the summit at 1.8 mi.

The most obvious feature in the summit view is Great Sacandaga Lake to the south and southwest, but to the northwest one can see Blue Mountain and Snowy Mountain, while Crane Mountain is prominent due north. On a truly clear day, one can see Algonquin Peak just to the left of Crane Mountain and Mt. Haystack and much of the Great Range just to the right. Contrary to what is shown on the viewing map in the brochure, Mt. Marcy is just hidden behind Crane Mountain.

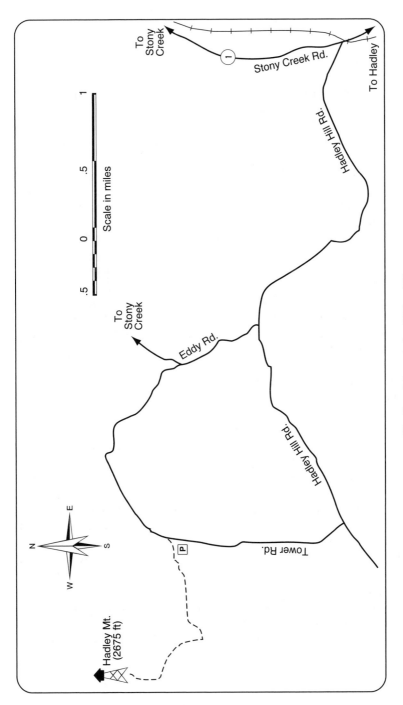

Hadley Mountain (Trip 42)

43. Murphy Lake from Pumpkin Hollow Road

Distance: 6.4 mi (10.3 km) round-trip
Difficulty: Ski, intermediate; snowshoe, novice
Maps: ADK Southern Region; USGS Three Ponds Mountain and
    Hope Falls metric series

Set in a deep valley, Murphy Lake is an attractive destination with a pretty lean-to at its southeast corner. The trail has one short steep spot, but otherwise it is quite skiable as it follows the route of an old stagecoach road. As is the case with most of the ski routes in this area, the surface of the trail is somewhat eroded and at least a foot of packed snow is required for the trail to be skiable (but still with rocks to dodge) and two feet is preferable. There is moderate snowmobile traffic on this route, but its narrow width serves to keep speeds low.

▶ The start is 1.5 mi from NY 30 near the end of Pumpkin Hollow Road, which turns east from NY 30 0.3 mi north of the sign designating the southern town line of Wells. At the start there are DEC signs indicating snowmobile trails heading both left to Pine Orchard and Wilcox Lake and right to Murphy Lake. The trail itself is marked with both yellow DEC and snowmobile trail disks. ◀

From the trailhead (0.0 mi) the trail descends a short, steep pitch at 0.2 mi (no hill on the route is any steeper than this pitch), but then is mostly flat to an unmarked junction at 0.8 mi. At this junction the Murphy Lake Trail bears left, followed by another sharp left at 1.0 mi. Soon the trail begins a moderate descent on a washed-out section of old road before leveling out and crossing Doig Creek on a wooden bridge at 1.6 mi. Now the trail climbs gradually to a crest from which the cliffs on Huckleberry Mountain can first be seen. A crossing (no bridge) of the outlet to Murphy Lake is reached at about two miles, above which the trail follows the shore of a large beaver pond. Continuing to follow the stream above the beaver pond, the trail comes to a second crossing of the Murphy Pond outlet—again without benefit of a bridge—at 2.4 mi. In good conditions, neither of these crossings should require more than normal care. (The second crossing is potentially more difficult, but can be avoided by skiing up a ridge to the outlet of the pond.)

After the second crossing, the trail proceeds up through a narrow ravine and reaches the west shore of Murphy Lake at 2.9 mi. The attractive lean-to on Murphy Lake is located about 0.3 mi along the southeast shore of the lake.

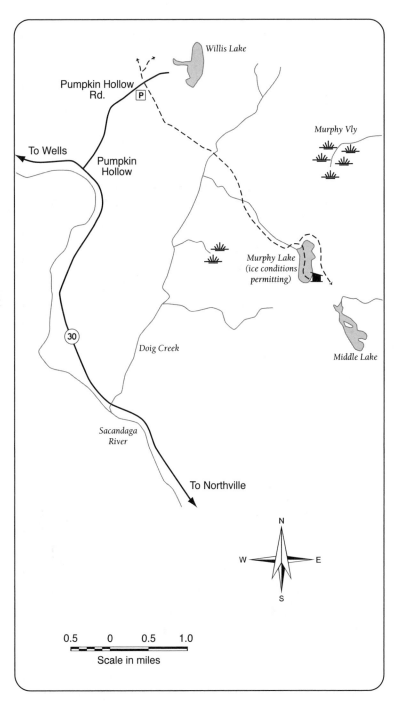

Murphy Lake from Pumpkin Hollow Road (Trip 43)

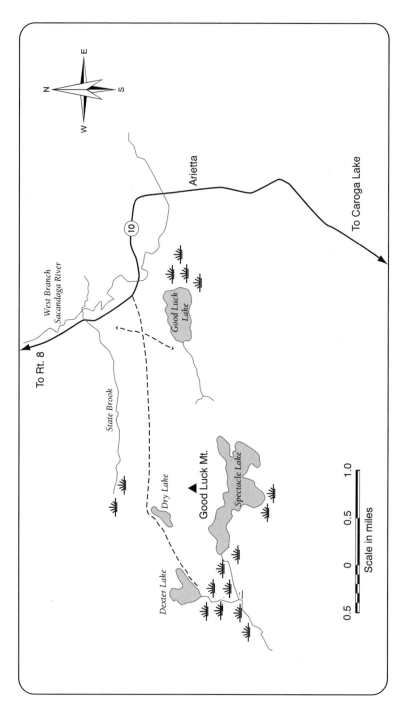

Dry and Dexter Lakes (Trip 44)

44. Dry and Dexter Lakes

Distance: 5.8 mi (9.4 km) round-trip
Difficulty: Ski, novice-intermediate; snowshoe, novice
Maps: ADK Southern Region; USGS Morehouse Mountain metric series
and Canada Lake 7.5' sheet

In addition to the two primary objectives, one can extend this trip with
a circuit through the marshes connecting Dexter Lake with Spectacle
Lake and return via the Spectacle Lake Trail for a round-trip of approximately 8.5 mi. The trail as far as Dry Lake is generally flatter and therefore less eroded than many of the other old roads in this area, making this a good choice if there is less than a foot of packed snow. There is, however, one steep eroded section getting to Dexter Lake.

▶ The start is on NY 10 just past the second bridge over the West Branch of the Sacandaga River north of the hamlet of Arietta. The trailhead is marked with a small DEC sign. ◀

From the road (0.0 mi), the trail climbs gently and then descends slightly to a crossing of a heavily used snowmobile trail at 0.5 mi. Beyond the snowmobile trail is a fork. (The trail left leads to Good Luck Lake.) Bearing right, the trail continues gently up and down, reaching a large wet area at 1.2 mi, a stream with an old bridge at 1.4 mi, and finally a view of Dry Lake at 2.1 mi. One can either keep to the trail or descend to the pond and ski to the west end at 2.3 mi. From Dry Lake the trail climbs gradually up into a ravine and then at 2.7 mi begins to descend a steep, rocky ravine to the shore of Dexter Lake at 2.9 mi.

Snowmobile markers continue beyond. The trail they mark is indistinct in summer, and without any recent snowmobile activity a map and compass is the only realistic method to proceed to Spectacle Lake and the possible round-trip. With recent snowmobile use, however, this route can be followed—using care not to follow just any track so that one will indeed arrive at Spectacle Lake.

Eastern Region

Comprised mostly of the terrain east of the Adirondack Northway (I-87), the Eastern Region offers numerous opportunities for shorter trips to a variety of interesting destinations. The longest trips are in the Pharaoh Lake Wilderness Area, the region's only designated wilderness area.

This region's major drawback for winter use is that its location on the east edge of mountains means it tends not to receive as much snow as the rest of the Adirondacks. Sometimes a coastal storm will track just right and the Champlain Valley will actually be about the only place in the Adirondacks to get snow, but usually the eastern Adirondacks has to make do with the "leftovers" of any storm. In a normal-to-above-average snow year this is not a problem, but some years have seen only a few days of skiable snow in many parts of this region.

There are no cross-country ski centers in the region where one can call to check on conditions. The Town of Schroon Lake, however, maintains some cross-country ski trails along with their snowmobile trail system.

Eastern Region Cross-Country Ski Sites
Schroon Lake 518-532-7675

Eastern Region

Trail Ratings for Skiers

Novice
50. Crane and Goose Ponds

Novice-Intermediate
45. Pharaoh Lake
49. Berrymill and Moose
    Mountain Ponds

Intermediate
46. Round Pond from Sharp Bridge
    Campground

Expert
47. Split Rock Mountain
48. Black Mountain (up and back only)

Trail Ratings for Snowshoers

Beginner
50. Crane and Goose Ponds

Novice
45. Pharaoh Lake
46. Round Pond from
    Sharp Bridge Campground
49. Berrymill and Moose Mountain Ponds

Intermediate
47. Split Rock Mountain
48. Black Mountain (up and back;
    see *Expert* entry below)

Expert
48. Black Mountain (complete loop; see *Intermediate* entry above)

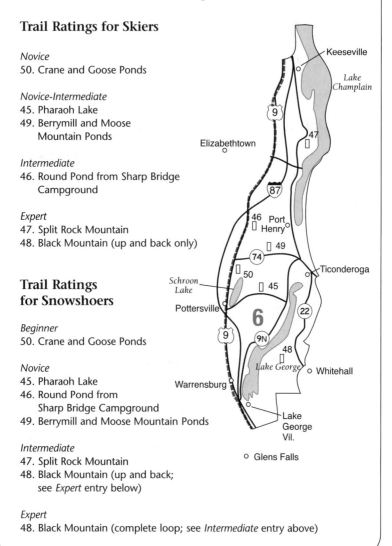

45. Pharaoh Lake

Distance: 8.0 mi (12.9 km) round-trip to south end of lake; 12.4 mi (20.0 km) round-trip to north end of lake
Difficulty: Ski, novice-intermediate; snowshoe, novice
Maps: Page 136. ADK Eastern Region; USGS Pharaoh Mountain 7.5′ sheet

This two-mile-long lake with several picturesque lean-tos along its shores is not only beautiful but also may claim the title as the largest Adirondack lake not reached by a road. The approach is via a long-abandoned woods road so that the skiing is generally easy. The distance to the lake is 1.5 mi longer in the winter than in summer, but skiers are likely to find this terrain so pleasant that they can consider the extra 3.0 mi a delightful bonus. This trip is in the Pharaoh Lake Wilderness Area, so snowmobiles are prohibited, although there has been some snowmobile trespass in recent years.

▶ To find the start, turn off NY 8 onto Palisades Road at the east end of Brant Lake (approximately six miles northeast of the hamlet of Brant Lake). From Palisades Road turn right onto Beaver Pond Road, which is the third road to the right at 1.5 mi from NY 8. Drive another 1.0 mi on Beaver Pond Road to the beginning of Pharaoh Lake Road on the right. Pharaoh Lake Road is now plowed for the first few hundred yards to some private camps, but parking is limited. Be sure to leave room for larger vehicles to turn around, and if there is any chance a snowplow will need to turn around, leave even more room by parking on Beaver Pond Road. ◀

From the parking at the end of Beaver Pond Road (0.0 mi), the trail is nearly level through a notch between Park and No. 8 Mountains to the wide valley of Mill Brook and the summer parking area at 1.5 mi. After crossing Mill Brook on a plank bridge, the trail soon begins to climb. At 2.0 mi the grade eases, after which gentle ups and downs lead to a bridge across Pharaoh Lake Brook at 2.7 mi. From this bridge, the trail climbs briefly and then levels out next to an extensive open area of beaver activity on the left. Continuing generally close to the brook, the trail reaches the south end of Pharaoh Lake at 4.0 mi. Although this is a good destination in itself, most will want to head up the lake, if ice conditions permit, at least as far as one of the several lean-tos along the shore. Continuing up the lake, one is rewarded with a rapidly widening view of the surrounding mountains the farther one goes. It is approximately 2.2 mi more to the lean-to at the north end of the lake.

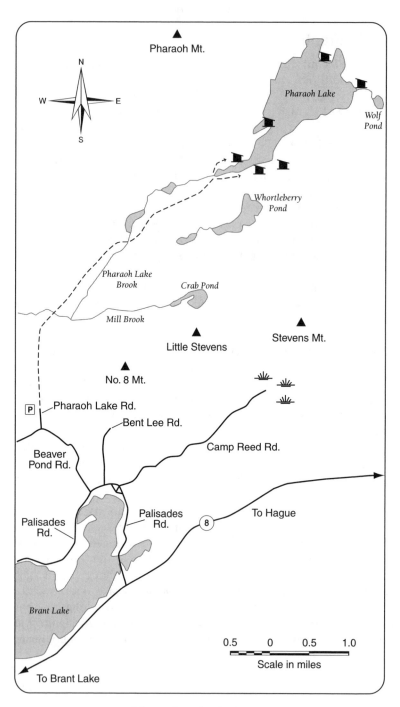

Pharaoh Lake (Trip 45)

46. Round Pond from Sharp Bridge Campground

Distance: 8.0 mi (12.9 km) round-trip
Difficulty: Ski, intermediate; snowshoe, novice
Maps: Page 138. ADK High Peaks Region; USGS Witherbee metric series

For most of its length, this trip follows an old wagon road known as the Cedar Point Road that was a significant transportation link in the early to mid-nineteenth century. It was by this route that loads of iron ore from the original mining operation at Tahawus were transported to Cedar Point on Lake Champlain near the present campground in Port Henry. After some years of neglect, this trail is again being regularly maintained and regularly used in winter.

▶ The start is at Sharp Bridge Campground on US 9, 7.1 mi north of the hamlet of North Hudson and 2.9 mi south of Exit 30 on the Northway. There is usually a small parking area plowed on the east side of the highway, but traffic is light on this section of highway and parking on the road should present no problem. ◀

From the road (0.0 mi) proceed to the far end of the field next to the river and find the register at the start of the red-marked trail, which follows the left bank of the Schroon River for 0.8 mi to an old bridge abutment. This was the original crossing of the Schroon River by the Cedar Point Road that by 1830 ran from Port Henry to Newcomb on a line north of the present Blue Ridge Road. A few years later the Great Northern Turnpike (the predecessor of US 9) began to share this crossing, which was used until a bridge was built at the present campground.

At this point, the trail turns sharp left and over a small rise to a new bridge across a small brook. Once beyond the brook, the route climbs a moderate grade to a pass at 1.5 mi after which it drops in two successive pitches to flatter going in a magnificent stand of white pines. Continuing mostly on the flat, the trail arrives at the south end of East Mill Flow at 2.7 mi.

The hiking trail turns right to cross the brook below the flow, but in winter one can usually use the ice to cross to the road on the east side or go up the flow for about 0.7 mi. At 3.4 mi the outlet of Round Pond crosses the old road and enters East Mill Flow, and just north of this point the road turns sharp right and climbs gently to a junction at 3.5 mi. Here the red-marked hiking trail turns sharp right, but the shortest route to Round Pond continues on the old road that, though overgrown, is easily followable and continues straight ahead, reaching the northwest shore of the pond in another 200 yd. There are some attractive rocks on a point on the north shore, which one can reach by following

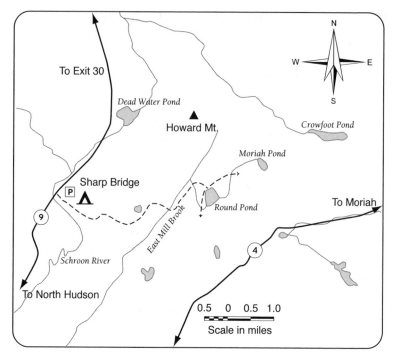

Round Pond (Trip 46)

the road and then a trail along the shore if ice conditions do not permit going straight across on the ice. The distance to the pond is 4.0 mi.

If time permits, two variations are possible that extend the trip and take in some additional scenery. From Round Pond, one can continue northeast on the old road for about a mile to Moriah Pond and its views of the rugged cliffs of Broughton Ledge. Another possible variation for the return is to go to the south end of Round Pond and head down the large marsh next to the outlet until it meets the hiking trail just above East Mill Flow. (The marked hiking trail leads past Round Pond and on to Trout Pond on the North Hudson–Moriah Road. This is a possible shorter approach for snowshoers, but is too rough to be good skiing.)

47. Split Rock Mountain

Distance: 3.2 mi (5.2 km) round-trip; 5.4 mi (8.7 km) loop
Elevation change: 670 ft (204 m)
Summit elevation: 1033 ft (315 m)
Difficulty: Snowshoe, intermediate; ski, expert
Maps: Page 140. USGS Westport and Willsboro metric series

Acquired by the State of New York in 1994, this spectacularly rugged ridge rising above Lake Champlain offers many possibilities. The loop described below takes in the highest terrain that has been developed to date, but there are many other old roads which lead to both lookouts and down to the lake itself that have yet to be cleared and marked. The current edition of *Adirondack Mountain Club High Peaks Trails* details more of the opportunities available on the Split Rock property.

Before the sale to the State, this property was heavily logged with the woods further damaged by the 1998 ice storm. Much of the forest is thus not very attractive, but the logging left behind an extensive network of roads, some of which have been pieced together to create this tour. There are many other logging roads that are not part of the trail system, so some care is required to be sure one is on the marked route. As the skiing difficulty rating indicates, there are some steep spots that will challenge even the best of skiers. Therefore, a 3.2 mi up-and-back snowshoe trip to the highest point may be, for many, the best way to explore this area initially.

▶ The start is on Lake Shore Road between Westport and Essex. From the junction of NY 9N and NY 22 in Westport, take NY 22 north for 0.4 mi and turn right onto Lake Shore Road. The parking area is on the right, 4.3 mi from NY 22. From Essex, go straight ahead on the main street instead of turning right on NY 22. This street becomes Lake Shore Road. The parking area is on the left at approximately 5.5 mi, 0.4 mi past the intersection with Clark Road. ◀

From the register (0.0 mi) the trail, marked with yellow DEC disks, climbs moderately past one side trail on the right at 300 yd to another junction at 0.3 mi. The marked route goes left and up a short, steeper pitch, after which the grade moderates to a junction with a blue-marked trail at 0.7 mi. (The yellow-marked trail makes a 0.2 mi loop that goes right and steeply up and over a small bump with some limited views before descending to a second junction with the blue-marked trail.) To avoid the side loop, take the blue-marked trail straight ahead for 250 yd to the second junction with the yellow-marked trail.

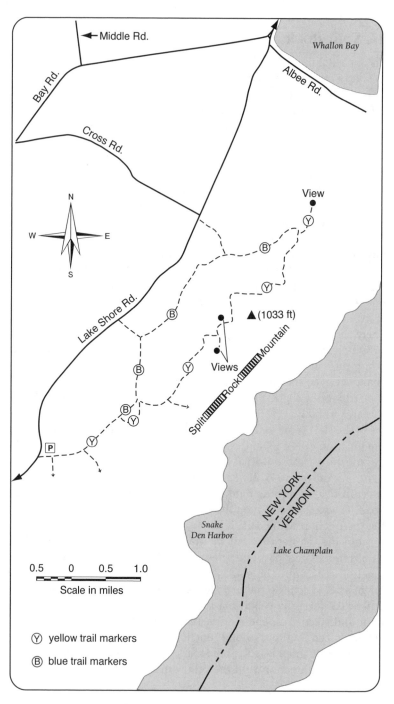

Split Rock Mountain (Trip 47)

Going straight, and again with yellow markers, the trail ascends gradually to a side road, right, at 0.9 mi. From here, a generally gradual climb leads to a saddle between two bumps at 1.2 mi. After a moderate descent, the trail now climbs steeply to the left of a large cliff and up to a junction in a saddle at 1.6 mi. The narrow trail at right leads approximately 250 yards to a spectacular lookout with Lake Champlain directly below and Giant Mountain and the Dix Range visible to the west.

To continue on the full loop, turn left and climb a short, steep pitch to another summit with a less expansive view to the west. From this summit, the trail descends over some rough terrain and then swings left on a smoother road and continues a moderate descent to a right turn across the hillside at 1.9 mi.

After briefly climbing again the trail continues to descend moderate grades down a ridge to a junction with the blue-marked trail at 2.7 mi. (The yellow-marked trail continues straight ahead for 0.2 mi to its end at a view looking north along Lake Champlain.) From the junction, the blue-marked trail goes west and soon begins a steady, moderate descent on a wider, but in places rougher, road to a junction at 3.2 mi. Here the blue markers go left. (This wider road descends at a slightly easier grade to Lake Shore Road at a point approximately 1.7 mi north of the parking area.)

Turning left with blue markers, the loop continues to descend gradually with some flat sections to a junction at 4.1 mi. (Here a turn to the right would lead to Lake Shore Road about one mile north of the parking area.) Turning left at the junction, the blue markers lead up gradual to moderate grades to the junction with the yellow trail at 4.6 mi. Turn right, still with blue markers for 250 more yards, after which the yellow trail is followed back to the parking lot, which is reached at 5.4 mi.

48. Black Mountain

Distance: 6.6 mi (10.6 km) loop; 5.0 mi (8.1 km) round-trip
Elevation change: 1046 ft (337 m)
Summit elevation: 2646 ft (854 m)
Difficulty: Snowshoe, intermediate (up and back), expert (complete loop); ski, expert (up and back only)
Maps: ADK Eastern Region; USGS Shelving Rock and Whitehall 7.5′ sheets

The complete loop as described below offers a variety of scenery and terrain, but the shorter up-and-back trip still offers the reward of some truly spectacular views of Lake George from the summit.

The loop trip starts on easy terrain and passes or crosses several picturesque ponds before presenting the snowshoer with a steady, but never too steep climb that is a good test of one's climbing technique. After a thaw-freeze cycle, instep crampons may be necessary for this final climb to the summit. The descent is an easy shuffle down an occasionally used snowmobile trail.

For skiers, the snowmobile trail has some challenging pitches but is a feasible route up and back to the summit. The trail on the south side of the peak is definitely not ski terrain, although a round-trip as far as Black Mountain Pond makes for a pleasant 6.0 mi novice-intermediate tour.

▶ The start is off NY 22 between Ticonderoga and Whitehall. Turn west at the sign for Huletts Landing and go 2.7 mi to Pike Brook Road. Turn left for 0.8 mi to a parking area on the right. ◀

From the register (0.0 mi) the red-marked trail follows an old road up a short moderate grade and then on easy terrain for 0.5 mi to a bypass around an old farmhouse and barn before reaching a junction at 1.0 mi. The trail to the right is the direct route to the summit and the return for this trip for those doing the loop.

Turning left and now with blue markers, the trail descends and crosses a brook on a bridge just below a beaver dam, after which a short moderate climb is followed by a gradual descent to the spur trail to Lapland Pond Lean-to at 1.9 mi. The lean-to sits on a picturesque point of rock on the north shore and is worth the side trip or can be a destination in itself. (Ice conditions permitting, those who go to the lean-to can go across the pond to the inlet and quickly regain the trail just before it reaches the junction with the Black Mountain Ponds Trail.)

Continuing past this junction with the spur trail, the route crosses the inlet to Lapland Pond and reaches a junction at 2.1 mi. Turning right here, the trail reaches Round Pond at 2.3 mi. Under most conditions,

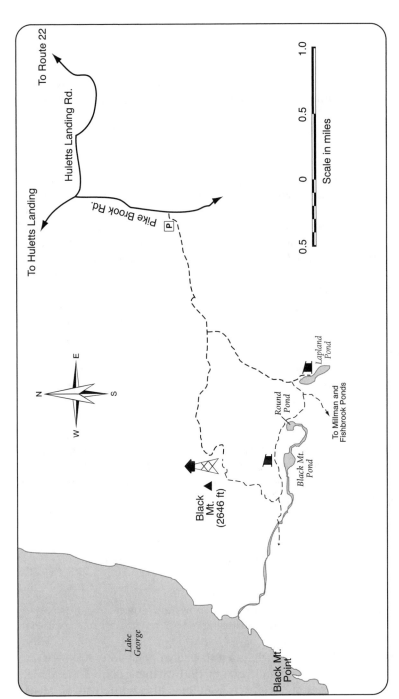

Black Mountain (Trip 48)

one can cross Round Pond on the ice and then follow the low, mostly open area that leads to Black Mountain Pond rather than following the trail that leads along the north side of the ponds. There is a great view of Black Mountain from the pond and this marks the end of the possible ski tour.

To continue toward Black Mountain, climb up to the right for a few yards at the west end of the pond to regain the trail, which reaches a junction with the Black Mountain Trail at 3.1 mi. Turning right here, one begins a moderate-to-steep climb with several switchbacks. Just past a rock wall on the right, the trail comes to the first of many lookouts at 3.3 mi. At 3.9 mi the grade begins to ease off with some open areas to the left. A short side trip here leads to the best views of the south end of Lake George. Continuing on and now mostly flat, the trail goes through several spruce thickets and reaches the summit at 4.1 mi. Just beyond the closed fire tower and communications equipment is a view of the north end of Lake George.

The return route starts by going down past the old observer's cabin and then following a mix of red hiking trail and snowmobile disks down into the trees. Because most winter users seem to follow the marked snowmobile trail, the return is described accordingly.

From the observer's cabin, both trails descend steeply for 0.2 mi. Here the red-marked hiking trail continues a steep descent while the snowmobile route traverses left across the face of the mountain to the north ridge. First dropping steeply off to the northwest for 100 yards, the grade moderates as the trail swings right and regains the crest of the ridge from which there are views of the lake. The snowmobile trail continues down several steep switchbacks with more moderate grades in between before reaching easier going and rejoining the hiking trail at just under one mile from the summit. Now it is a mostly gradual downhill to the junction with the Lapland Pond Trail and the return to the start at 6.6 mi.

49. Berrymill and Moose Mountain Ponds

Distance: 6.2 mi (10.0 km) round-trip
Difficulty: Ski, novice-intermediate; snowshoe, novice
Map: USGS Paradox Lake 7.5' sheet

The destination for this trip is a little-known pond accessible on a trail constructed from Berrymill Pond in 1991 by inmates from the Moriah Shock Incarceration Facility. A lean-to at the north end of Moose

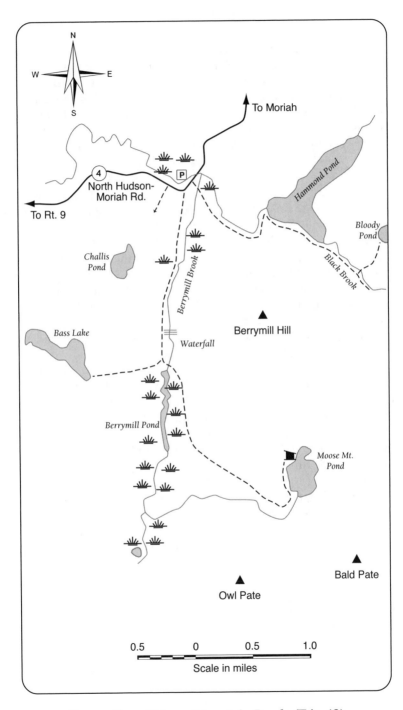

Berrymill and Moose Mountain Ponds (Trip 49)

Mountain Pond further enhances the trip, and this was one of the destinations for the Centennial Challenge sponsored by the Adirondack Park Visitors Interpretive Center in 1992. From the lean-to and the low cliffs nearby, one can see Moose Mountain and Owl Pate from a perspective that makes them appear far higher than their low (2000 ft) elevations would indicate. There is also a possible side trip to Bass Lake and an adjacent tour to Hammond and Bloody Ponds to round out the opportunities for short, relatively easy trips in this area.

▶ The start for all these trips is on the North Hudson–Moriah Road, which runs east from US 9, north of North Hudson. Coming from either the north or south on US 9, signs for Moriah and the Champlain Bridge direct one onto an old section of US 9 from which the North Hudson–Moriah Road branches east. It is 2.9 mi from this point to the trailhead at a large turnout on the south side of the road. One must be careful as the trail to Challis Pond branches off less than 0.1 mi before this trail; and the trail to Hammond Pond starts less than 0.1 mi east of the Moose Mountain Pond trail. The Moose Mountain Pond trail is marked with blue DEC disks. ◀

Heading practically due south (as opposed to southeast for Hammond Pond), the trail reaches the edge of a marsh at 0.3 mi. A new bypass trail goes right and up, but in winter the best route is to follow the old road through the marsh and then up until the bypass trail returns from the right at 0.7 mi. One now climbs gradually past a small waterfall to a junction with the trail to Bass Lake at 1.3 mi. Bearing left, the trail soon crosses a new bridge over the outlet to Berrymill Pond. (The pond and marsh extend south for about one and one-half miles and make an interesting side trip.)

After crossing the bridge, one slowly climbs away from the pond, heading southeast and finally northeast through mature pine and hemlock forests to the south end of Moose Mountain Pond at 2.9 mi. The trail continues along the west shore, but the easiest traveling, ice conditions permitting, is across the pond to the lean-to at 3.1 mi.

50. Crane and Goose Ponds

Distance: 4.6 mi (7.4 km) loop
Difficulty: Ski, novice; snowshoe, beginner
Maps: ADK Eastern Region; USGS Paradox Lake and Graphite 7.5' sheets

The two destinations described here make for some pleasant going without having to rely on favorable ice conditions.

▶ From the flashing light at the junction of US 9 and NY 74 off Exit 28 in Schroon Lake, proceed east on NY 74. About one-half mile after crossing the Schroon River, turn right on South Road, and in another 0.6 mi turn left on Alder Meadow Road. Proceed 0.9 mi, then turn left on Crane Pond Road, which is plowed for another 1.5 mi to a parking area at the boundary of the Pharaoh Lake Wilderness Area. ◀

In the summer of 1991, the DEC officially closed the road beyond this point and erected a barrier to prevent vehicular access, but those who wanted to preserve motorized access to Crane Pond soon removed the barrier. As a result, there is some snowmobile trespass to Crane Pond and beyond.

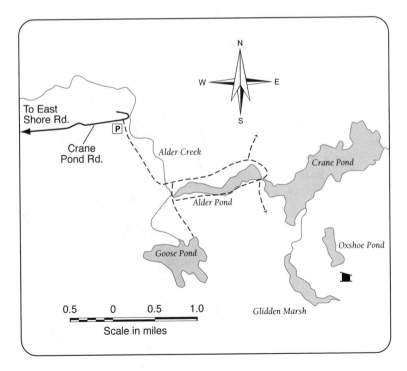

Crane and Goose Ponds (Trip 50)

From the parking area at the end of the plowed road (0.0 mi), one climbs gently to a bridge over Alder Creek at 0.7 mi, and then descends slightly to a junction with a trail, right, to Goose Pond at 0.9 mi. This is the return for those doing the complete circuit as described. Continuing toward Crane Pond, the road goes over a ridge and down, passes a trail left to NY 74 at 1.7 mi, and reaches the end of the road at Crane Pond at 1.9 mi.

To continue to Goose Pond, cross the bridge over the outlet to Crane Pond and then turn right to ski along the wide and open shoreline of Alder Pond to the Goose Pond Trail at 2.7 mi. (Alder Pond is primarily a beaver pond, and the open shoreline is the result of many years of higher water levels. If the beavers have reflooded the pond, backtrack to the marked trail.) Turning left on the Goose Pond Trail, one goes gradually up through a magnificent hemlock forest to the top of the hill at 3.0 mi. For skiers the most significant aspect of this forest is not its magnificence but the large amount of room between the trees in which to maneuver on the descent.

From the top of the hill, a short gentle descent leads to the north shore of Goose Pond at 3.1 mi. There is a nice open bluff to the right with a view of Pharaoh Mountain. This can be reached either along the shoreline or by going across the pond if ice conditions permit. The return to the start by the Goose Pond Trail and Crane Pond Road is 1.5 mi, for a total trip of 4.6 mi.

BETSY TISDALE

About the Author

Raised in Hartford, Connecticut, Tony Goodwin was introduced to the Adirondacks as a child through summers in Keene Valley, New York. He began skiing downhill at age six and cross-country at age seventeen. Goodwin first snowshoed in 1966 when he attended the ADK Winter Mountaineering School. He returned the following year to  the school's Advanced Leadership Section and subsequently served as an instructor for four years in the Adirondacks and on Maine's Mt. Katahdin. He holds a B.A. and an M.A. in History from Williams College and the State University of New York at Plattsburgh, respectively.

His position as venue manager for the Lake Placid Olympic Organizing Committee led to his appointment as manager of the Mt. Van Hoevenberg cross-country ski area in 1981. After five years at Mt. Van Hoevenberg, he left to help found the Adirondack Ski Touring Council, which constructed the twenty-four-mile Jackrabbit Trail, and was also named Executive Director of the Adirondack Trail Improvement Society.

An Adirondack Forty-Sixer, Goodwin has been the editor of ADK's authoritative *Guide to Adirondack Trails: High Peaks Region* and of the accompanying map—through three editions and numerous reprintings—since 1984. In addition, he served on the High Peaks Wilderness Citizen's Advisory Committee, which provided ideas for that region's Unit Management Plan. He has long filled an informal role as an educator-spokesperson on recreational issues confronting the High Peaks, and has done so with humor and tenacity. Goodwin is the author of two previous ADK ski touring guides, *Northern Adirondack Ski Tours* (1982) and *Classic Adirondack Ski Tours* (1994), and of numerous articles for *Adirondack Life, Adirondack Explorer,* and *Adirondac.*

Backdoor to Backcountry

ADKers choose from friendly outings, for those just getting started with local chapters, to Adirondack backpacks and international treks. Learn gradually through chapter outings or attend one of our schools, workshops, or other programs. A sampling includes:

- Alpine Flora
- Ice Climbing
- Rock Climbing
- Basic Canoeing/Kayaking
- Bicycle Touring
- Cross-country Skiing and Snowshoeing
- Mountain Photography
- Winter Mountaineering
- Birds of the Adirondacks
- Geology of the High Peaks ... and more!

For more information:
ADK Member Services Center
(Exit 21 off the Northway, I-87)
814 Goggins Road, Lake George, NY 12845-4117

ADK Heart Lake Program Center
(near Adirondak Loj on Heart Lake)
P.O. Box 867, Lake Placid, NY 12946-0867

Information: 518-668-4447
Membership: 800-395-8080
Publications and merchandise: 800-395-8080
Education: 518-523-3441
Facilities' reservations: 518-523-3441
E-mail: adkinfo@adk.org
Web site: www.adk.org

Join Us

We are a nonprofit membership organization that brings together people with interests in recreation, conservation, and environmental education in the New York State Forest Preserve.

Membership Benefits

- **Discovery:**
  ADK can broaden your horizons by introducing you to new places, recreational activities, and interests

- **Enjoyment:**
  Being outdoors more and loving it more

- **People:**
  Meeting others and sharing the fun

- ***Adirondac* Magazine**

- **Member Discounts:**
  20% off on guidebooks, maps, and other ADK publications; discount on lodge stays; discount on educational programs

- **Satisfaction:**
  Knowing you're doing your part and that future generations will enjoy the wilderness as you do

- **Chapter Participation:**
  Brings you the fun of outings and other social activities and the reward of working on trails, conservation, and education projects at the local level. You can also join as a member at large. Either way, all Club activities and benefits are available.

Membership
To Join

Call **800-395-8080** (Mon.–Sat., 8:30 A.M.–5:00 P.M.), visit **www.adk.org**, or send this form with payment to:

Adirondack Mountain Club
814 Goggins Road
Lake George, NY 12845-4117

Check Membership Level:

- ❏ Individual $50
- ❏ Family $60
- ❏ Student $40
  (full time, 18 and over)
- ❏ Senior (65 or over) $40
- ❏ Senior Family $50
- ❏ Lifetime Individual $1300
- ❏ Lifetime Family $1950*

School _____

*2 adults residing in same household—not transferable.
Multiyear memberships are also available.

Fees subject to change.

Adirondack
ADK
Mountain Club

Name _____

Address _____

City _____ State _____ Zip _____

Home Telephone ( )_____

- ❏ I want to join as a Chapter member*
- ❏ I want to join as a member at large

For family memberships, list spouse and children under 18 with birthdates:

Spouse _____

Child _____ Birth date _____

Child _____ Birth date _____

Bill my: ❏ MASTERCARD ❏ AMERICAN EXPRESS ❏ VISA

Exp. date _____ Sec. Code _____

_____

_____
Signature (required for charge)

* For details, call 800-395-8080 (Mon.–Sat., 8:30 A.M.– 5:00 P.M.)
Or visit www.adk.org

ADK is a nonprofit, tax-exempt organization. Membership fees are tax deductible, as allowed by law. Please allow 6-8 weeks for receipt of first issue of *Adirondac*.

SST

ADK List of Publications

FOREST PRESERVE SERIES

1 Adirondack Mountain Club High Peaks Trails
2 Adirondack Mountain Club Eastern Trails
3 Adirondack Mountain Club Central Trails
4 Adirondack Mountain Club Western Trails
5 Adirondack Mountain Club Northville–Placid Trail
6 Adirondack Mountain Club Catskill Trails

OTHER BOOKS

Adirondack Alpine Summits: An Ecological Field Guide
Adirondack Birding: 60 Great Places to Find Birds
Adirondack Canoe Waters: North Flow
Adirondack Mountain Club Canoe and Kayak Guide: East-Central New York State
Adirondack Mountain Club Canoe Guide to Western & Central New York State
Adirondack Paddling: 60 Great Flatwater Adventures
An Adirondack Sampler I: Day Hikes for All Seasons
Catskill Day Hikes for All Seasons
Forests and Trees of the Adirondack High Peaks Region
Kids on the Trail! Hiking with Children in the Adirondacks
No Place I'd Rather Be: Wit and Wisdom from Adirondack Lean-to Journals
Ski and Snowshoe Trails in the Adirondacks
The Adirondack Reader
The Catskill 67: A Hiker's Guide to the Catskill 100 Highest Peaks Under 3500'
Views from on High: Fire Tower Trails in the Adirondacks and Catskills
Winterwise: A Backpacker's Guide

MAPS

Trails of the Adirondack High Peaks Region
Northville-Placid Trail
Trails Illustrated Map 742: Lake Placid/High Peaks
Trails Illustrated Map 743: Lake George/Great Sacandaga
Trails Illustrated Map 744: Northville/Raquette Lake
Trails Illustrated Map 745: Old Forge/Oswegatchie
Trails Illustrated Map 746: Saranac/Paul Smiths
Trails Illustrated Map 755: Catskill Park

ADIRONDACK MOUNTAIN CLUB CALENDAR

Price list available upon request, or see www.adk.org.

Index

Locations are indexed by proper name with *Camp, Lake,* or *Mount* following.

Notes